SCOTTISH WOMEN'S · STUDIES SERIES ·

Upstairs
— to —
Downstairs
Advice to Servant Girls and Weary Mothers

Extracts from the magazine of the
Onward and Upward Association

Selected and introduced by
James Drummond

ABERDEEN UNIVERSITY PRESS

First published 1983
This edition published 1991
Aberdeen University Press

© James Drummond 1983

British Library Cataloguing in Publication Data
Drummond, James
   Upstairs to Downstairs
   1. Home economics—Great Britain
   I. Title   II. Onward and Upward Association
   640'.942   TX145

   ISBN 0-08-041204-1

PRINTED IN GREAT BRITAIN
THE UNIVERSITY PRESS
ABERDEEN

FOREWORD

I am pleased and proud to write a foreword to Mr James Drummond's excellent book. When I first came to Haddo House at the end of the War a copy of 'Onward and Upward' and 'Wee Willie Winkie' was thrust into my hand by Ishbel Aberdeen's old secretary, Georgie Mackenzie. It meant little to me then but as I learnt more about my illustrious predecessor, (frequently incidentally being asked to do the kind of nursing medical work which she had done—her case of special medicines etc. were preserved—and for which I was singularly unqualified!) I came to realise what an advanced thinker she was, and so far ahead of her time. The ecumenical Chapel and the Hall built in the time of 'We Twa' bear witness to this.

That she was unpopular, particularly with her own class of society, I knew—but this does not detract from her greatness. Her children revered her but were fearful of her. Her grandchildren were not and loved her dearly for her sense of youthfulness and fun was akin to theirs. She was a very forceful woman—she did not like to be called a lady!—as all great innovators must be and took her more gentle husband along with her in all these schemes. And how many schemes there were, all of which had to be financed largely by their own purse, and Haddo House Estate was virtually beggared in the process. But all these schemes were for the betterment of mankind, and the ordinary people loved her and were grateful.

As for the Hall, which was opened by Moody and Sankey of evangelistic fame, and which was the centre and heart of the Haddo House Club, it flourishes more than ever under the benign ownership of the National Trust for Scotland, as a Community Centre and apart from the music is used for all sorts and kinds of activity. Auchedly and Ythanbank WRI, one of the first and founded by Ishbel, now meets there, and Sunday School picnics still go on all through the Summer. All of which would be very dear to her heart. And if today the helpful hints and the stories and advice of 'Onward and Upward' make us smile we should remember how much that is good that has happened since then is due to great innovators such as 'We Twa' in whose long and happy married life so much was achieved.

June Aberdeen & Temair

v

CONTENTS

ACKNOWLEDGEMENTS

I am grateful to June Gordon, Marchioness of Aberdeen and Temair, for her interest in this project, for the help and encouragement she has given and for her permission to use various family papers as source material.

I also thank Mrs M B Longley, Secretary of the Haddo House Choral and Operatic Society, for her careful arrangements in the Muniment Room and for helping me to find my way through the books and documents there; I am grateful to Mrs A Gauld, the Factor's Secretary, and to Miss R Dickie, Lady Aberdeen's Secretary, for the many ways in which they have helped.

It was very pleasant, and very useful, from time to time to set aside the documents and letters and to have a chat with Mr Dawson Henderson about life on the estate in bygone days. My thanks to him.

Sincere thanks are also given to my good friend, Miss Mary Towns, for her lively interest in this venture and for all her careful work in preparing the typescript and reading the proofs. I am also grateful to Mrs Ann Mackie and Mrs Emily Scott for helping with the typing.

I gratefully acknowledge the help given by the Staff of the Local Collection of Aberdeen Central Library, Mrs Elma Garden, Miss Isabella Deans and Miss Catherine Taylor. My thanks also to the Librarian and Staff of Aberdeen College of Education Library, and to the Staff of the National Library of Scotland.

Finally I wish to thank both my wife, for her help with the research for the book and for correcting the typescript and proofs, and Colin MacLean who first suggested to me the idea of putting this book together. His help and advice have been invaluable.

Note: The extracts and illustrations have been gathered from the 1891–6 issues of the magazine *Onward and Upward*. The extracts have been grouped according to subject. The titles of these subject groups were suggested to the Editor by phrases, title-headings, etc. in the magazine.

JD

INTRODUCTION

A man's position in Society could be measured by the number of servants he employed and the quality of the service at his dinner parties. Greatest household of all was of course Buckingham Palace where on state occasions servants outnumbered guests at a ratio of two to one and the cost of one plate of consommé would have kept a working-class man and his family well fed for two days or more.

At the lowest end of the social scale were the unfortunates who had to make do with a young and inexperienced maid of all work and the laundry sent out. Off the social scale altogether were the working classes, from whose ranks servants were recruited. Country girls were preferred because they generally had more stamina than the urban proletariat and were less likely to have ideas above their station.

A man who could afford a male servant, however young, was clearly coming up in the world: when he engaged his first butler he had arrived. A good butler did more than attend to the smooth running of the household. It was he, and the housekeeper, who established in the servants' hall those high standards of propriety and deference so necessary for the comfort and convenience of the family and their guests Upstairs.

Indeed it was very often the butler and the housekeeper who engaged new servants. They knew the particular qualities to look for. Since knee breeches and stockings were part of the livery of the footman it was important that he have well-shaped calves. Tall parlour-maids were very much in fashion. They should be good looking but not so much so as to invite the attentions of the male members of the family. If she lost a front tooth she was liable to drop £2 in the salary scale, or even be demoted to housemaid.

A housemaid needed physical strength and deft fingers, a kitchen-maid an equable temperament under pressure. Scullery maids were called 'slaveys'. The next step up was a 'tweenie' so called because she divided her time *between* scullery and kitchen. A slavey or a tweenie needed, above all, enough energy to keep her going from 5.30 a.m. until midnight and the ability to 'hold her tongue' and to 'know her place', that place being the very lowest rung of the strictly regulated hierarchy of Downstairs.

The larger the household the more strictly defined were the duties of each grade of servant. For a footman to set a fire or carry coal would be as improper as for a page-boy to dust the nick-nacks in the drawing-room. In many households meals in the servants' hall were almost as stiff and formal as the dinner parties Upstairs. Butler and housekeeper sat at the top, scullery maid and boot boy at the bottom. After the first

1

course had been eaten the Upper Servants would retire to the housekeeper's room where the other two courses would be served to them. In some households the lower servants were not expected to join in general conversation until their betters had withdrawn.

A complex system of narrow passageways and back stairs separated the servants' quarters from the part of the house where the family lived. Some of the more stately homes still enforced the rule that if any servants below the rank of footman met the Master in a corridor, they should turn and face the wall until he had passed. To save the family the inconvenience of learning the servants' names, standard names were given to particular ranks. The first footman was usually 'James' while 'Margaret' was considered suitable for a parlourmaid. The upper servants were called by their surnames unless these were considered either vulgar or pretentious.

It was incorrect to say 'please' to a servant but 'thank you' was permissible as an acknowledgment of a task cheerfully and expeditiously performed.

Thanks to the 1870 Education Act most servants could now read. Between 1890 and 1904 no fewer than forty-eight new weekly or monthly magazines appeared specially aimed at the servant class. 'Times are changed', wrote the editor of *The Servants' Magazine*. 'Servants are fond of reading, but it is of vast importance that what they read should be adapted to suit their real welfare, to render them useful in their station, more contented with the arrangements of a kind Providence which has placed them in it.'

At first sight the magazine *Onward and Upward* seems to fall into this category of piously condescending propaganda designed to persuade the servants that their best interests lay in sticking to their duty instead of taking themselves off to the greater freedom of office or factory. But first impressions can be deceptive: during the period (1891–96) when the Countess of Aberdeen was the editor and from which the extracts in this book are taken, *Onward and Upward* was no ordinary magazine; its editor was no ordinary Countess.

Ishbel Marjoribanks, daughter of Lord Tweedmouth; married in 1877 to the Earl of Aberdeen, Peer of the Realm and successively Lord High Commissioner of the Church of Scotland, Lord Lieutenant of Ireland, Governor General of the Dominion of Canada. The family seat was Haddo House, Aberdeenshire, and in accordance with the requirements of the Season they spent much of the year at their town house in Grosvenor Square. They had over a hundred servants and knew them all by their own names. Ten footmen and not a 'James' amongst them. This was an unfortunate eccentricity, but there was worse to follow. There were strange stories about the Earl swopping jokes with the butler in the pantry; about the scullery maids and the tweenies getting bed-time cups of cocoa from Lady Aberdeen; about members of the family playing hide and seek along those very corridors which should have kept Upstairs at a proper distance from Downstairs. The stories were not accurate, but there was enough truth in them to damage the Aberdeens' social position. To such an extent ultimately that King Edward VII refused to stay in the Viceregal Lodge when he visited the Lord Lieutenant and his Lady in Dublin 'in case he found himself obliged to take a parlourmaid in to dinner'.

*   *   *

Before her marriage, Ishbel Marjoribanks had busied herself with 'rescue work' amongst young prostitutes in the Strand district of London. Her parents, horrified, asked their great family friend Mr Gladstone to dissuade her, but instead he encouraged her. Indeed when he was forced by political pressure to give up his own 'practice' he asked Ishbel to look after a number of young street walkers whom he had been trying to help. With one at least of these girls she was successful (see the fifth letter extract on page 86).

Now, as Mistress of Haddo House, she was determined to carry the rescue operation into the farmlands of Buchan. There was much need. Below stairs in the big houses butler and housekeeper kept a watchful eye on the young servants, while the 'no followers' rule and the nine o'clock curfew in the smaller establishments kept many a girl out of mischief. It was far different in the farmhouses. In Aberdeenshire it was the custom for girls to leave home and go into service as soon as they were thirteen. The ones who could not get jobs as domestics in private houses went to work on the farms, living in servants' quarters near the farmhouse, helping both in the farmyard and in the kitchen. The young male farm-hands lived in the 'chaumers'—outhouses, attic rooms or bothies—eating their meals and taking their leisure in the kitchen along with the girls. It was a rough, free and easy atmosphere, far different from the protective formality and strict decorum of the servants' hall.

On the servants' annual holiday they would pour into the nearest market town and, according to one of the local clergymen, would indulge in the kind of 'drunken horseplay that many hitherto innocent young servant girls would, in due course, have a life-long cause to regret'. The bothy ballads were not only very shocking: they were also true.

In the August of her first year as Mistress of Haddo House, the young Lady Aberdeen invited every domestic and farm servant in the neighbourhood to a garden party in the grounds of Haddo instead of going on the traditional spree. Nearly six thousand of them accepted the invitation and were served with tea, lemonade and cakes by Lady Aberdeen and those of the mistresses who, with some misgivings, had agreed to help. Despite prophecies of riot disorder and drunken vandalism the whole thing went off very well and the *Scotsman* newspaper had a leading article about the experiment 'so notable for its novelty and success in these days of conflict between classes'.

So if the elevating influence of the gentry could be brought to bear on the lower orders on one day of the year, why not oftener and in a more systematic way? A community centre was built in Methlick and farm servants were invited to continue their education by coming to evening and Saturday afternoon classes in arithmetic, reading and geography. An encouragingly large number of boys and young men from the neighbouring farms were glad enough to come to the classes and as the Countess' volunteer helpers grew more confident in their ability to make contact with the young people, more kinds of activities, educational and recreational, were organised.

The trouble was that few servant girls attended the classes. 'The mistresses all and one agree that they cannot think of allowing their girls out, for they are sure to get into mischief', wrote Lady Aberdeen to her mother. 'The morality of the girls is something terrible.'

She tackled the problem by organising what was in effect a forerunner of the Open University of our own day. If the girls could not come to the educational centre, they would study during their free time in their own kitchens. They were invited to join what was called the Haddo House Association. Every Associate was sent work schemes and reading lists for any two of the subjects on offer. The most popular were arithmetic and reading, but biology came a close third. What distinguished this venture from ordinary correspondence courses was a tutorial system organised by district committees who were also responsible for assessment and certification. The key figures were the mistresses themselves who were expected to help the girls with their studies, lend them books and supervise the examinations.

The educational aims were of less importance than the social one of giving middle-class mistresses and working-class girls a common interest. This, it was hoped, would improve working-class morality by precept and example. To make more explicit the purpose of the exercise, Associates were asked to promise that they would try to lead lives of temperance and purity.

The Association flourished. By the end of its first year it had enrolled eight hundred girls and five hundred mistresses. Attempts to amalgamate with the Scotch Girls Friendly Society broke down over the refusal of Lady Aberdeen to accept the G.F.S. 'Central Rule' whereby a girl who 'surrendered to temptation outside Christian marriage' also surrendered her membership card.

Perhaps because of this more tolerant attitude, by 1891 the Haddo House Association had spread so far throughout Scotland that its name was no longer appropriate and various alternatives were considered. *Victoria League* with the motto 'I will be good' was a possibility as was *Lily Band* 'in the hope that the emblematic character of the flower and the care with which it has to be cherished may prove an inspiration to some young lives'. Finally they chose the name *The Onward and Upward Association,* 'because', wrote its President, 'it explains what we aim at—the opposite of Backward and Downward'.

The whole thing may seem slightly ludicrous nowadays, but there was nothing to smile at in the 1890 police report, that four out of five of

Aberdeen's 180 prostitutes were former domestic servants and that most of them could expect to be dead within four dismal years of taking up their new occupation. The way Backward and Downward was indeed a grim one: it was high time for it to be reversed. To accomplish this Lady Aberdeen decided to publish a monthly journal dedicated to the ideals of the Association.

The magazine *Onward and Upward* was therefore a magazine with a Purpose. Much of the inspiration—and of the editorial policy—came from the popular theologian Henry Drummond. Lady Aberdeen herself described Drummond as 'the closest of our friends and comrades. What I owe to his friendship is more than I can ever hope to express'. Her daughter, Lady Marjorie, said that he was 'a beacon light illuminating the whole current of her life'. It was the Countess' boast that his sermon 'The Greatest Thing in the World', probably the most widely read sermon of the century, was first preached to the Aberdeen family and their servants in the Chapel of Haddo House.

Henry Drummond did more than perhaps any other man of his time to help people reconcile their religious belief with the disturbing and controversial findings of modern science. Darwin had proved the biblical theory of the creation of the world to be wrong. Drummond's message was that this should bring hope, not despondency. Just as biological evolution was still continuing, so was man's spiritual evolution, so that ultimately we would reach the material and spiritual perfection immanent in the Creation.

This optimistic faith in Progress appears on every page of *Onward and Upward*: the linking of material and spiritual progress does a lot to explain the curious mixture of household hints and moral aphorisms, of economical recipes and 'improving' stories. The magazine reflects Drummond's faith that the Smallest Things in the world are often the greatest. Every kind action, every generous thought, every increase in the joy and comfort of the humblest home is a step onward and upward in the pilgrimage to a better world.

The serial story 'Her Day of Service' is a good example of this comfortable philosophy. Drummond, by means of an article in the *Spectator,* had supplied Lady Aberdeen with the guidelines for the writing of stories of an elevating nature for servant girls. 'Cultivated ladies of leisure will be delighted to find out the marvellous power exercised by a writer who likes girls and who likes books. Working girls want kind, cultured friends and simple tales in which they can find their own lives mirrored in a pure and friendly light. It is worth stooping if lives can be brightened and improved by showing little kindnesses and trivial tales. Small things lead to great: our fires of coal will burn solidly and brightly enough if only they can be lit with light rubbish.'

Mrs Isabella Fyvie Mayo's light rubbish 'Her Day of Service' appeared in the same year as Thomas Hardy's great novel *Tess of the d'Urbervilles*. If they are both taken on the same level simply as social documents the comparison is not ludicrous. They share the same

theme—a simple country girl is forced by family misfortunes to leave
home and go into domestic service, where she has to cope with new and
sometimes difficult situations. Mrs Mayo's heroine Margaret Ede is an
embodiment of the belief that in a girl's innocence lies her safety.

> So wise in all she ought to know
> So ignorant of all besides

She therefore passes from girlish innocence to virtuous and fruitful
marriage without any intervening ordeal of anguish and uncertainty.

Hardy's Tess also starts off on life's adventure with all the attributes
of an onward and upward girl: the catalogue of her misfortunes
therefore illustrates Hardy's social pessimism, his refusal to accept the
faith that the world is ordered in such a way that we are likely to
achieve happiness by certain rules of behaviour. By contrast *Onward
and Upward* is infused with this Victorian belief that there *is* a certain
formula for happiness: all that is needed is for the formula to be
packaged and passed on to the mass of mankind. For Charles Dickens
the formula was humanity; for Henry Drummond it was practical and
joyful Christianity; for *Onward and Upward* and an entire generation
of reformers and philanthropists it was a mixture of both, well diluted by
a large dose of the middle-class ethic; diligence, honesty, self-denial and
all the other conventional virtues set out so clearly for the readers of
'Her Day of Service': a kind of self-activating agony column for girls
who wanted to get the formula right.

The other key figure during the early days of the *Onward and Upward*
magazine was W T Stead, pioneer of modern journalism. He too believed
in the power of the well-told story to improve the lot of mankind. In 1885
his 'Maiden Tribute to Modern Babylon' in the *Pall Mall Gazette* had so
disturbed public opinion that a reluctant Parliament was forced to rush
through a law raising the age of consent from thirteen to sixteen. But
there was still much to do for the protection of young girls: in the editor
of *Onward and Upward* he found an energetic ally. Lady Aberdeen had
the magazine produced in London where the new technology of
printing, based on cheap newsprint, mechanical typesetting and the
rotary press could produce a large number of copies at a low cost. The
children's supplement *Wee Willie Winkie* under the nominal editorship
of Lady Marjorie beat the *Rainbow* to the starting line in the children's
comic race by quarter of a century.*

Stead gave advice on high-powered distribution techniques. He
arranged free transportation of the new magazine to hundreds of girls
who had recently emigrated. By 1897 there were 115 branches of the
Onward and Upward Association, four of them in Canada. Just before
the outbreak of the Boer War a new branch was started up at Isomo in
the Transkei: 'Pambili na Pezulu' is Kaffir for 'Onward and Upward'.

On editorial policy Stead had two pieces of advice. Firstly, the public
do not want to read about the 'women's rights movement': articles about
the emancipation of women would cut circulation figures drastically.

* *Ally Sloper* was for adults: *Funny Wonder* for office boys and kitchen-maids.

Lady Aberdeen was a strong supporter of the 'women's rights' movement but she took Stead's advice. As President of the Liberal League she continued to demand votes for women. As petitioner to the General Assembly of the Church of Scotland she demanded the admission of women to the ministry. But as Editor of *Onward and Upward* she kept in line with the moderate view expressed in the popular jingle—

> The Rights of Women: what are they?
> The Right to labour, love and pray
> The Right to weep with those that weep
> The Right to wake while others sleep.

'What we demand', she proclaimed, 'is the right to do our duty.'

Stead's second piece of advice was that any articles or stories about sexual morality must be well muted. He knew what he was talking about. For the alleged obscenity of his 'Maiden Tribute' story, Stead had been jailed for three months. Thomas Hardy was so appalled by the ferocity of the attack on him about 'Tess' that he gave up novel writing. Mrs Isabella Fyvie Mayo got off unscathed and wrote many more trivial but improving tales.

But if Lady Aberdeen was obliged to be timid on paper she was all the more determined to be bold in action. As President of the International Council of Women she pushed the issue of the 'white slave traffic' so frequently and forcibly onto the agenda that, as soon as there was an international organisation with enough muscle to do something about it, it was done. Perhaps the League of Nations' curbing of the white slave trade was its most effective and efficient operation. The long build-up that ensured this success had begun many years previously with the co-operation of Lady Aberdeen and Mr Stead in the production of *Onward and Upward*.

*   *   *

In the meantime, back at Haddo House, Lord and Lady Aberdeen had begun the interesting experiment which was later to bring them into Royal Disfavour. They had confessed to 'an uneasy feeling on our parts that while we were engaging in various philanthropic movements and trying to bring elevating influences to bear on the lives and surroundings of servants in other households, we were doing nothing to promote common interests amongst the members of our own household'. All their servants were invited to a meeting at which it was unanimously agreed that a club be formed. It would be the responsibility of an elected committee of eight to organise activities for the club under the two headings of Education and Recreation. Any fears that the butler and the housekeeper may have had about the subversive influence of democracy in the servants' hall were allayed by the results of the first election of the Committee: Lord and Lady Aberdeen were unanimously elected President and Vice-President respectively. The other members were all Upper Servants, and included the butler, the head gardener and the

Earl's valet. The under-butler, who wrote a beautiful copperplate, was chosen as secretary and treasurer. They called it the Haddo House Club.

Education was catered for by classes in elementary science, Bible study, composition and arithmetic. James Robertson (stables) proposed a class in Latin: he had no seconder but at least his proposal was minuted. It was possibly the first time he had spoken above a deferential mutter to his Betters in the servants' hall.

The development of the club's activities can be traced in the minute book so carefully kept by the under-butler. At their first social evening the President sits at the head of the table, flanked by butler and housekeeper. All the other servants sit in their allotted places. But at the next meeting 'Fred Hurst (odd job) strongly objects to the stiff way in which the Social met on Thursday. If possible to get small tables and to mix freely.' Which they do.

At the first Annual General Meeting it is agreed that 'in order to improve and educate members, more books be made available' and so sets of books are placed in the bothies, stables and the gun-room. Two copies of the evening paper will be placed in the Library with a ruling that 'a member could not retain a copy beyond ten minutes if another member of the Club required it'. A further serious breach of the discipline and hierarchy of Downstairs was made by the provision that all Club members would take their turn in setting and lighting the fire in the library on a Saturday afternoon.

When Lord Aberdeen moves to his town residence for the session of Parliament he takes the household with him and the Club assumes the name 'Grosvenor Square Club'. In Ottawa or Dublin Castle it is 'Government House Club'. As Governor-General and Lord Lieutenant he has to do a lot of entertaining as does Lady Aberdeen at the request of the Liberal Party Whip. Dinners and receptions are on a lavish scale and all the elaborate rituals must be strictly attended to. But there is an interesting innovation which, to begin with, is considered by the best people to be not quite the done thing, but which gradually wins acceptance even in smart circles. Many years later a Society journalist recalls how 'Lady Aberdeen was the first London hostess to break up dinner parties into groups of eight or ten and seat them at separate tables so that conversation could be more informal. Thanks to her, the long dinner parties that were so often a weariness of the flesh no longer flourish.' For this welcome release generations of diners surely owe a debt of gratitude to Fred Hurst (odd job) and to Maggie Gall (housemaid) who seconded his proposal.

Back at Haddo at the end of the Season the Club resumes its social activities. In the Chair, Mr G. Germain (under-butler). A pleasant evening was enjoyed by all.

Song 'Only a Pansy Blossom'	Annie Dunlop (housemaid)
Lecture 'Railways'	Lord Aberdeen
Whistling Solo	Hugh Smith (stables)

Cantata 'The Life of Lord Shaftesbury'	Singing Class
Piano Duet	Lady Marjorie and Miss Forssman
Song 'A Boy's Best Friend is his Mother'	John Keddie (page)

With practice came confidence and the discovery of much hidden talent. The Singing Class grew in numbers and soon they were ready to put on their first public concert, made possible by the enterprise of Lord Aberdeen who, on his return from Ottawa, brought with him blueprints for a hall, a replica of the community centres built for isolated townships of Canada. It still stands at the side of Haddo House, its walls decorated with the many souvenirs which His Excellency the Governor General and his Lady brought back at the end of their term of office.

The Club made full use of the new accommodation. For dances guests were 'requested to bring dancing boots as nailed boots would injure the floor of the New Hall'. But heavy boots were needed to get there—or one of the new safety bicycles—because people were making long journeys to what was rapidly becoming a community centre for the district. There was a full house, in wintry conditions, on New Year's Eve 1897 for what must have been the first ever home video show, a sequence of tinted slides on the Magic Lantern depicting the pathetic Tale of *Biddy, an Irish Servant Girl* while the Singing Class provided incidental music. Against this background of sound and light the text of the story was read by Mr Duthie (head-footman) "in a most feeling and touching way which brought tears to the eyes of many mothers. Mr Duthie is so thorough in all he does."

Stories about the activities of the Haddo House Club caused unfavourable comment in the drawing rooms of Park Lane and Belgravia. A gossip columnist wrote about 'the curious innovation the Aberdeens had introduced in their household. Once a week they changed places with the servants and waited upon their domestics at dinner.' Queen Victoria instructed her Prime Minister to investigate reports that her Governor-General in Canada was in the habit of dining in the servants' hall. Rosebery was able to reassure the Queen that all was well and that all the correct details of protocol were being followed, but he had to admit that there *was* a servants' club, that His Excellency had been elected President by a show of hands in the servants' hall and that the under-butler was secretary.

The Prince of Wales and the 'Marlborough House Set', always jealous guardians of whatever social conventions contributed to their own pleasure and comfort, were quite clear in their minds that the Aberdeens were letting the side down. A Conservative MP noted with some dismay the sinister fact that Lord Aberdeen had banded his domestics into a union in the same year as the great London Dock Strike and the setting up of the first Domestic Servants' Trade Union. Outraged hostesses attributed the growing insolence and restlessness of their own domestics to the bad example that was being set elsewhere.

'We learned to shrug off the hostility of Conservatives, Irish gentry and smart Londoners', wrote Lord Aberdeen. But both he and Lady

Aberdeen were saddened by distorted stories about their strange ménage and, by inference, the quality of their hospitality. It was at this time that jokes about the meanness of Aberdonians began to circulate widely and became the stock in trade of comedians and joke columnists until, about sixty years later, they were displaced by jokes about a different ethnic group.

In 1902 appeared a play by J M Barrie about a nobleman who insists that once a month the servants in his London residence come upstairs to the drawing-room to be served with afternoon tea by the members of his family. His wife, Lady Agatha, declares that 'it is his solemn duty as a Peer of the Realm to elevate and ennoble our servants, and that the best way of doing this is to treat them as our equals—not every day, you know, but once a month'. There was an icy correspondence between Lord Aberdeen and J M Barrie on the subject, but no action was taken.

The Admirable Crichton was well received, although one critic wondered whether Barrie was aware of 'the immensity of his attack upon the constituted social order of Great Britain'. The review in *Punch* proclaimed it 'pure fantasy' but came up with a more than usually rich crop of patronising jokes and cartoons about the social and intellectual pretensions of domestic servants.

The King did not see the funny side. He still remembered, with royal displeasure, how Queen Alexandra, presumably following the example of the Aberdeens, arranged on the day of his crowning that ten thousand female servants be invited to halls all over London where, as acknowledgement of all their hard work in preparation for the Coronation, their mistresses poured them cups of tea, handed round the sandwiches and cakes and did their best to converse with them in an agreeable manner.

Perhaps he was reminded of this dangerous experiment in 1907 when preparations were being made for his State Visit to Ireland. Unfortunately the Court Society Review had recently carried a report that the Lord Lieutenant had invited all the servants of his household to a ball which was opened by his wife, Lady Aberdeen, this being 'probably the first instance of a Lady Lieutenant descending from the pedestal of her dignity to inaugurate the amusements of her dependants'. The King decided that it would also be the last. Orders were given and Lord Aberdeen was informed that the King would not, after all, stay in Dublin Castle during his visit. In dismay Lady Aberdeen asked the Prime Minister to try to persuade the King to change his mind. Edward sent his host and hostess a curt autographed note, 'I look on it as a settled matter that we live on board the yacht.' One of his aides was heard to remark that presumably the servants would not be obliged to cancel their evening classes because of the King's visit.

The Aberdeens were welcomed back from Ireland by a Grand Concert in what was still called the 'New Hall' in spite of the fact that the redwood timbers had now been seasoned by more than twenty Buchan summers and winters. It was now regarded by the people of the district as a place where those in no way connected with the estate could occasionally join in with the Haddo House Club to exercise their talents as singers, actors and instrumentalists. So for this welcome-home concert the Singing Class was supplemented by about thirty singers and players from neighbouring farms and villages. Music making at Haddo was becoming an important community enterprise.

The concert was held on a warm summer evening in 1914. Nobody realised that for the Haddo House Club, the Onward and Upward Association and many other good and worthwhile things it was 'the end of an auld sang'.

After the Great War everything was different. The Onward and Upward Association dwindled away, many of its functions being taken over by mixed youth clubs and, for the older ones, the Women's Rural Institute. The magazine had stopped publication by 1930. The Haddo House Club, its membership much reduced both by the war and by the financial embarrassments of its President, was formally disbanded when Lord and Lady Aberdeen had to move to Cromar House. There they wrote their joint-autobiography *We Twa*. There can be few public figures so long and so often engaged in political and social controversy whose reminiscences are so entirely free from rancour, self-justification and personal recrimination. The earl died in 1934. Busily involved in public life to the very end, Lady Aberdeen was responsible for the Peace Pavilion at the 1937 Empire Exhibition. She died just before the outbreak of the Second World War.

*   *   *

The television cameras follow the great soprano on her farewell tour. After the glittering magnificence of the New York Metropolitan, the sunlit elegance of Glyndebourne, and the scarlet and gold of the Royal Opera House, Covent Garden, the view up the drive at Haddo, Aberdeenshire, gives a pleasant feeling of homecoming. But there is no sense of anticlimax: the quality of the performance is as commanding as anything one could hope to find in the grandest of concert halls. For everybody gathered in the hall, audience and performers alike, it is clearly a very special experience. Janet Baker looks relaxed in the happy and orderly surroundings of Haddo House, rejoicing in the immediate warmth of the rapport with her audience. Some of them have travelled far to hear her but for many it has been a short journey, for the people of the neighbourhood still look on Haddo as being a kind of community centre, a feeling perhaps strengthened by the fact that Haddo House now belongs to the National Trust and is rapidly becoming one of the most popular of the Trust's properties in this part of Scotland.

Some of the magic of the music comes from the hall itself. The timber roof, carefully stressed by the designer to withstand the fury of the Canadian winters, gives back a resonance that adds the touch of perfection. Surely too, much of the magic comes from choir and orchestra, responsive to every tilt of the conductor's baton. The conductor is the Marchioness of Aberdeen and Temair, better known throughout the musical world as June Gordon, Musical Director and Conductor of the Haddo House Choral and Operatic Society.

In his book *The Music of the North* Eric Linklater describes how June Gordon and her late husband, the Marquess of Aberdeen, began the society as a purely local venture. 'They developed in their neighbours a capacity of which these neighbours had previously been unaware, and by nursing unsuspected talents they have enriched their neighbourhood . . . nothing much mattered except enthusiasm, camaraderie, a useful voice or a tender touch on the strings . . . a responsive ear: these were the qualities the Gordons looked for in the recruits who came so doubtfully at first to the doors of Haddo House. These great doors were thrown open and Haddo has become the centre of a creative and truly communal activity.' The *Sunday Times* music critic also felt the unique atmosphere at Haddo: 'There is something very special about music making at Haddo House, an involvement of amateur chorus, professional musicians and receptive audience that is both spiritually and mentally refreshing.'

When and how did this very special thing begin? Was it that day in 1945 when the new master of Haddo House, David Gordon, grandson of 'We Twa', following a kindly precedent, sent a message Downstairs inviting servants and estate workers to form a Singing Class with his wife June as Conductor? Or was it in 1947 when the choir that had begun in this informal, almost casual way was first stunned and then elated when June and David Gordon proposed that they reach for the stars and put on a public performance of the *Messiah* with solo artists of international repute?

Or perhaps we should go back exactly fifty years earlier when, at a meeting of the Haddo House Club, as recorded in the minutes for 19 January 1897: 'Mr Clark (odd job) suggested that the Committee think over matter as to the advisability of the Singing Club getting up a first class Concert to give the district the opportunity of hearing some really good Artists.' At the time Mr Clark's proposal was defeated in favour of an evening of 'Cinematograph Entertainment with moving Photographs of Humorous, Pathetic and Celebrated Events reproduced on the Screen with Actual Movements of Life'. If Mr Clark could have foreseen that the timber walls of the New Hall would some day resound to the music of such 'really good Artists' as Vaughan Williams, Peter Pears, Alexander Gibson, Janet Baker and June Gordon, he would perhaps have thought that his proposal had not, after all, been rejected and that he and the other members of the Haddo House Club had brought to this corner of Buchan something more enduring than flickering shadows of Celebrated Events on a silver screen.

What are the Objects of our Association

by Lady Aberdeen (1891)

The story of the 'Onward and Upward Association' is well known amongst ourselves yet we must once again trace its history for the benefit of new readers of our monthly Magazine.

To begin with it was called the 'Haddo House Association' because it was there that, in December 1881 a number of ladies, nearly all of them wives of tenants on Lord Aberdeen's estates, met together to discuss what could be done to raise the standard of living amongst the young women, especially the servant girls, in that part of the country.

We recognised that unhappily many influences have been steadily at work of late years which have tended to make servants keep together as a class and indeed to look upon their interests as opposed to, instead of identical with, those of their masters and mistresses.

We also agree that, although we had been led to form a high estimate of the Aberdeenshire servants, there were certain matters relating to language and behaviour which left much to be desired. We concluded that the following were some of the reasons:

1 Want of home training, and often lack of proper arrangements for the servants at their place of work.

2 The practice of frequently changing places, which prevents mistresses from taking an interest in their servants and which prevents the girls from settling down to their work and taking a pride in it. The changing of places engenders a restless selfish spirit and accustoms the farm servants in particular not to mind the coarse ways and usages of the feeing market and such like places.

3 The monotony of a servant's daily life. Nothing but a routine of work and very few outside interests to enliven it except the gossip and stories of the kitchen.

4 The language too generally used and some of the periodicals and stories too commonly read.

We desired to reach mistresses as well as servants and to bind both together by common interests. We wanted to make our aim elevation of women materially, mentally, morally—to help all who joined us 'Onward and Upward', which was the motto we adopted and which has recently become the new name for our Association.

We desire ever to remind our members of the sanctity of the body as

13

well as of the soul. We meet the young girl from school and urge her to begin her life's work with a high idea of the values of a woman's virtue, to aim to keep it unspotted in word, in look and in deed; we desire to encourage and help those who are battling on nobly with daily life, monotony and temptations. But at the same time we do not want to shut out those who have fallen, but rather to pass on to them the word of forgiveness and restoration. We decided therefore that there should be no rule of exclusion whatsoever. All are made welcome. The 'Scotch Girls Friendly Society' is doing a noble work to uphold the standard of purity. But I think that it needs by its side another Society which has no rule qualifying for admission and in which a member who loses her character is not required to forfeit her card.

But by the same token we give a set of clothes or a cot to the first child of every associate who marries and on whose former life there is no blemish. In this way we seek to point out that the sin repented of can be entirely forgiven and that the sinner may be wholly restored, but that in the marriage of one who has been kept pure there is a beauty and a blessedness not otherwise attainable.

For this reason Rule 4 of the Association is 'to endeavour to lead a life of temperance, of truthfulness, of purity and love and to do my daily work as in God's sight'.

We endeavour as far as possible to do all we can through the mistresses so as to bring them and their servants together through some common tie, out of which all manner of sympathetic feelings and needs and acts may arise. We therefore send out to the mistresses during the winter, papers of questions for the girls on Bible, history, geography and general subjects, and we offer also prizes for needlework and knitting and writing. The papers are all done at home by the girls and are examined in every parish by a local committee and each associate who averages eighty-five marks per paper receives a prize.

The papers are by no means given principally for the sake of education, but as a link and means of intercourse between members and associates; through these papers they get to know each other. The girl may come and ask her mistress for help or may request the loan of a book; the mistress takes an interest in the girl's answers and then each may begin to know more of one another's life and thought and a kindlier feeling is evoked. The questions should give the girls an interest beyond their every-day life and may lead them to read good books and may provide both occupation and material for conversation in the evenings.

Then we try to introduce a 'fashion' for remaining on in the same situation by offering prizes for periods of service of two, six, ten and fifteen years, the prizes increasing in value according to the length of service.

As we worked on we became convinced that the great cause of all we lamented was chiefly in the want of a high tone in the homes where our girls had been brought up and in the want of early training. They enter early womanhood with no knowledge of the temptations awaiting them.

They are without a reverential hallowed awareness of all that is involved in the words 'love', 'betrothed' and 'marriage' and are accustomed to hear such matters made the subjects of joking and 'chaffing'. And so, full of the high spirits of youth, with no definite aims, unaccustomed to self control, they proceed to do as others do; they do not mean to do anything wrong, but simply to take what amusement they can, and courting is a fine amusement so they go into it as into a dream, from which they awake too late, to find their lives for ever overshadowed with a dark remembrance.

We felt therefore that if we were to attain our object of gradually raising the conception of womanhood amongst the young women, we must induce their Mothers to help us in our work. We all acknowledge that it is in their hands that the power lies. It is the mother who is the regulator of the home life. It is her words and ways which must be the main influence in the lives of the little children, for a working man can of necessity see little of his children—it is she who is responsible for the household arrangements of the family, and if she regards the safeguards of virtue which are necessary for the well-being of the family all will be well. But if she creates or tolerates conditions that are favourable to vice, as only too often occurs in working-class homes, the germs of evil will not fail to fructify.

The problem was how to reach the mothers? We decided that the best way was to enroll 'married associates' as well as 'single associates' in the 'Onward and Upward Association'. These married associates would be asked to accept and sign a card of membership. In order to make it easier for the mothers to join they were not asked to bind themselves to anything more than to aim at keeping a few short rules as follows:

1   To begin and end each day with prayer.

2   To endeavour to lead a life of temperance, truthfulness and purity.

3   To guard my tongue from all scandalous and improper conversation.

4   If children are given me, to do all in my power to guard them from contact with evil, and from hearing improper conversation.

5   To prevent them from reading bad books and periodicals.

6   To endeavour to learn about ways that will conduce to keeping my husband, my children and myself in cleanliness, comfort and good health, and that will enable me to nurse them in case of sickness.

7   To remember the sacredness of marriage and ever to make home a bright place for my husband and children.

The cards on which the rules are printed can be obtained for a small sum from Messrs Wyllie, Union Street, Aberdeen. They are prettily illuminated with a design of snowdrop or ivy, and many of the married associates frame them and hang them up in their homes, the mere possession of the card being thus a silent witness in the home.

'A mother's work is never done.' Night and day she must be ever ready for the sick child, the noisy boys, the fretful baby or the weary husband, and when there is no change, no relaxation, it must be difficult to be always cheerful and loving and to remember the high aims which she would wish always to keep before her. Many mothers rarely get out of the house but must stick to the monotonous round of duty, so monotonous that she forgets that all great achievements are brought out by constant attention to small and tiresome details, and that it is by teaching little habits of decency, purity, industry, honour and thought for others in a bright and happy home that she is preparing her children to live grand lives. Her children may not be conscious of the training, but in after years memories will come back to them of the atmosphere of that home, which will preserve them from evil and cause them to call their mother's name blessed.

Ladies have said to me 'I would feel as if I were interfering if I broached on such subjects as are mentioned on the card', but if we approach them as mother speaking to mother, both anxious for their children's welfare in this world and the next, many an encouraging word may be frankly spoken, and undoubtedly we shall learn as much as we teach. The lives of working women have much, much to teach us.

It is always inspiring to think that we belong to a great body joined together for the attainment of an object which should uplift every word and action of our common life. It is our earnest hope that this Magazine may stimulate and make us realise our responsibilities in belonging to a great Family bound together by common ties.

Helpful Hints for Willing Workers

As I write to you, dear Readers, hard working mothers and honest servant girls, I fancy I can see around me thousands of faces young and old who have grasped the white banner which we have unfurled and on which gleam the golden letters 'Onward and Upward'.

In the pages of this, the monthly journal of the 'Onward and Upward Association' you will find, we hope, pleasure and relaxation for your leisure hours. Of much greater importance, however, are the bits of advice and guidance. Some of them will be plain work-a-day hints on how to go about your household duties, either as a servant or as a working mother. Alongside these household hints you will find items that are meant to guide your hearts and minds to more serious matters. There is no real strangeness in this mixture, for to a woman her responsibility to the family which she tends and her sense of higher things surely form a seamless web of dedication to Duty.

> The trivial round, the common task
> Should furnish all we ought to ask
> Room to deny ourselves—a road
> To bring us daily near to God.

The kitchen table should be scoured daily or more often if necessary. The boards must be scrubbed with the grain, not round and round as so many careless girls like to do. Use a paste of sand, soft soap and lime.

In washing linen, if pipe-clay is dissolved in the water the linen is thoroughly whitened with half the labour.

When brushing a carpet always work towards the fireplace and in this way a good deal of dust disappears up the chimney.

Vigour, energy, resolution and devotion to our duty, however humble: these carry the day.

Rinse fish knives and forks under the cold tap before washing in warm water. This helps to get rid of the fish taint.

17

Save spent tea leaves for a few days then steep them in a pail for half an hour: strain through a sieve and use the tea as a detergent to cleanse all varnished paints.

When wax candles become dull and yellow they should be cleaned with methylated spirits.

To purify sinks add one pound of sulphate of iron to four gallons of water and pour some down the sink three or four times a day.

The greatest wrong a man can do a woman is to take from her her duty and dedication and self denial.

Spots on silver spoons should be removed by rubbing with a little fine whitening damped with ammonia.

Ceilings which have become smoked with paraffin lamps should be washed with soda water.

Blacking for boots mixed with stale beer gives an extra and more lasting brilliancy to the polish.

A parlour maid who will lay the table with smudgy glass and spotted china cannot be a good Servant and the sooner she is told to go the better for the comfort of the household.

Dainty Dishes for Slender Incomes

Porridge is delicious if it is lightly sprinkled with hard grated cheese instead of sugar.

Stewed peas for sixpence

$\frac{1}{2}$ peck green peas (cost 4d), 1 teacup white sugar, 1 teaspoon flour, 2 tablespoons water, 1 onion, 1 oz butter, 1 sprig mint (2d). Put in stewpan butter, water, sugar, mint, onion; stir till boiling and add peas. Stew gently till soft. Remove onion and mint. Mix flour with cold water and stir into peas. Boil for three minutes and serve.

Caledonian cream

2 tablespoons red currant jelly, 2 tablespoons sifted sugar, whites of 2 eggs. Switch together for half-an-hour.

Savoury dumpling

Scald and wring $\frac{1}{2}$ lb bread. Mix it with 1 lb of flour, 5 oz of dripping, 2 oz of chopped onion, one teaspoonful of mixed herbs, and half a saltspoonful of pepper. Boil three hours in a cloth.

Rice and treacle

Boil half a pound of rice till quite tender; turn it out in a wire sieve; drain, and then half fill some teacups (or tumblers) with it, pressing it down neatly, so as to make all the same size. Stand them in cold water to set them, then turn out on to a dish and pour round them some treacle.

Macaroni pie

Any kind of cold meat finely minced, pepper, salt, a little Worcester sauce, an onion cut up small, and half a cupful of stock; place this mixture at the bottom of a pie-dish, fill it up with macaroni, previously well boiled and drained. Strew the top with grated cheese and little dabs of butter; bake in a brisk oven till the macaroni begins to colour.

Artificial cream

Stir a dessert-spoonful of plain flour into a pint of new milk. Simmer very gently to take off the raw taste of the flour.

Vegetable goose

Soak half a pound of breadcrumbs in cold water. Chop a large onion fine and mix with them. Add one teaspoonful of chopped parsely and mixed herbs, two ounces of butter, and pepper and salt. The bread should have the water well squeezed out before the other ingredients are added. Butter a shallow baking-dish, put in the mixture, and bake for about an hour in a good oven. Cut in squares and serve hot.

Bread balls for soup

Cut the crumbs of a stale loaf into small pieces, put them into a basin, and pour over them enough hot water to moisten without making them too wet; let them cool. Chop an onion, lay it in the frying-pan with a large lump of dripping and some chopped parsley, and fry a light brown; mix with the bread, and when cool add two well beaten eggs, salt, pepper, and sufficient flour to bind. Make the mixture into small balls, drop them into the boiling soup fifteen minutes before serving.

Lemon syrup

1 English pint lemon juice, 1 quart water, 4 lbs crushed sugar, 1 ounce tartaric acid. Boil the sugar in one-half of the water, and dissolve the tartaric in the other half. When cold mix together.

Sheep's head

Split open the head, and remove the tongue and brains. Soak the head after this in a little warm salt and water. Tie the two halves together, and bake the head in an oven for about a couple of hours, basting with butter or dripping. Boil the tongue separately, and make some brain sauce by boiling the brains, then mashing them up with a teaspoonful of mixed sweet herbs, and some butter, pepper and salt. Stir these brains over a gentle fire for some little time in a stewpan. Place the brains round the tongue, and serve in a separate dish from the head.

Carrot jam

Scrape and boil the carrots till tender, then smash them, and to each pound of pulp allow three quarters of a pound of loaf sugar and a pinch of ginger or any spice liked—something of the kind is necessary if the jam is to be enjoyed—and boil as for ordinary preserves.

Healthy Ways bring Happy Days

A Capital Chest Preserver: There is no better protection from wind and cold than a newspaper folded double across the chest inside the coat or waistcoat, the coat being buttoned over it.

Be on guard against the physical and moral dangers of an over-heated home. Reflect that the hot climate of the tropics makes the inhabitants of these regions indolent, weak and enervated so that they are easily subdued by invaders from the temperate zones, who are strong and vigorous and so rule the world.

The skin of a boiled egg is the best remedy for boils. Carefully peel it, wet and apply to the boil.

To cure a bad cold take five drops of camphor on sugar before going to bed at night.

Every window in the house should be thrown open for at least ten minutes twice a day and oftener if need be.

For Neuralgia in the face apply a mustard plaster to the elbow.

Remember the wise saying 'Feet warm, head cool, bowels regular—laugh at the Doctor'.

Sprained Ankle: Pound some caraway seed and heat it with a little water until it thickens. Apply with a bandage.

Bad Smells can ruin a life. If in the house there is a bad drain, too many in one room, or general neglect of things to make bad smells, then the family will suffer. They wake up in the morning feeling as tired as when they went to bed. Many a working man crawls from his bed in this state and when he comes to those shops that sell stimulants, is it any wonder that he is tempted? It is in this way that many who die drunkards begin to drink.

For Inflamed Eyes and Styes take a large baked potato, scoop out the inside and bind it over the lid on going to bed.

To take the Heat out of Chilblains bathe with a mixture of vinegar and salt which has been heated until it is painfully hot.

SICK-ROOM NURSING

It is a common error to ask minutely how a sick person feels. If they are better they will tell you so, and if not it is best not to remind them by asking.

Keep the sick-room cool by wringing long pieces of cotton out of water and hanging them before the open window.

Nurse Florence Nightingale writes that 'cream, as food for an invalid, is quite irreplaceable by any other article whatever. It seems to act in the same manner as beef tea or stewed tripe and many people prefer it.'

When comforting an invalid always look hopeful, never despairing. Do not contradict even the most fanciful thoughts. If the sick one thinks the curtain is green when it is really blue, what harm is there in allowing him to think so?

If the invalid asks you to read the newspaper aloud to him, omit the death-list and 'in memoriam'.

Grains of Gold to give a Lift on Life's Way

The great cure for Discouragement is a full persuasion of being in the path of Duty.

Selfish people always think their own discomfort of greater importance than the discomfort of others.

A Reader tells how she went downstairs to the kitchen and found the kitchen-maid on her knees on the red tiled floor. She had scoured the floor clean and was now rubbing it over with a piece of flannel soaked in skimmed milk in order to make it look polished and glossy. 'Doesn't it make your poor arms ache, Nelly?' she asked, and got the answer, 'Yes ma'am it do. But oh ma'am, see how lovely the floor looks!'

The worst wheel of all is the one that creaks and groans as it goes about the work of turning.

For cleaning wall-paper, stale bread is very good.

To choke down grumbling think, firstly, that many others are a great deal worse off than you are and, secondly, think how much of your difficulty is your own fault.

Constantly choose to want less rather than to have more. Never envy others and imagine that they are any the happier for having more of the good things of life.

Claret stains on fine table linen should be removed by holding the soiled part in milk while it simmers for twenty minutes.

Just one word to the girl who is downhearted, who is tired and whose life is filled with labour—Hope. If you keep on hoping from day to day and from week to week you will never feel entirely unhappy, and if with the Hoping you do some Helping you will be quite happy.

Cultivate the spirit of taking a cheerful interest in the simple round of daily life.

For scrubbing stone floors mix sand and soft soap with coarse whitening.

What is Duty? The demand of the hour.

Consider how much more you suffer for your anger and sense of grievance than for those very things for which you are angry or grieved.

Never say anything about anybody unless you are quite sure that it is true. If you are, then ask yourself why you want to tell it.

Common snuff put into the chinks of the fireplace will drive away beetles and crickets.

Think of those women who have enriched the world with story and song—have they not all been singularly domestic women, so that their genius has taken form from their womanly household lives? And so it may be with you.

Gas stoves should be thoroughly washed with hot water and soda and then rubbed vigorously with a little kerosene.

Cultivate the Garden of your Mind

There are many hours during the winter months which are full of weariness for servant girls and which are felt by some of those who have an interest in their welfare to be fraught not only with emptiness but also with evil, and the desire is to occupy those hours profitably and innocently.

You should strive to keep a corner of your life for some book of weight and worth—the works of our great poets—Scott, Tennyson, Wordsworth and Milton, or some of our histories or biographies. You might think it beyond you to master any of these but you should not let any such thought discourage you. You may have a very busy life and may not be able to call any hour entirely your own, but try to snatch a few minutes every day for the reading of one of those good and weighty books.

To me the highest type of true womanhood is exemplified in the life of a loving, patient, devoted wife or mother whose whole life is so apportioned and divided that she fulfils all the duties of a perfect wife and mother without starving her intellect and nature.

Every servant girl in the Onward and Upward Association is encouraged to study one or two Subjects and to take part in monthly written Examinations for which marks will be given and Prizes awarded.

HISTORY

Give a list of the Stuart Sovereigns of Scotland till James VI and tell (1) the relation of each to the preceding sovereign, (2) the age of each at the beginning of the reign, and (3) the manner of death.

Which English King hid in an oak tree and for how long?

What experiment was made by a Scottish King to find out the original language of mankind?

PHYSIOLOGY

What parts of the body can be compared to a boiler, an engine and machinery respectively?

Is it wise to pick the wax out of your ears with a pin? Give the reason for your answer.

Mention some examples of sociality in the brute creation.

In what various ways could you tell whether a person lying down with the eyes shut was alive or dead?

Describe the changes in the brain produced by education.

Can you think of any advantages in having so many of the parts of the body in pairs?

BIBLE KNOWLEDGE

Mention any two persons in the Bible who impress you as having been grumblers. Quote two texts warning us against a grumbling and discontented spirit.

Describe the battle fought by the Israelites against Amelek at Rehphidim.

Give from the life of Moses examples of (1) his meekness and (2) his firmness.

What injunctions against Waste are given in the Bible and how can they be applied in our daily work?

HOME HEALTH AND COMFORT

What is the best thing to do if we have the suspicion of bad smells or if we think there is something wrong?

Why is healthiness in the home even more important for women and children than for men?

Give two useful ways of using up stale cheese.

What is the first step to real reformation of character?

What is absolutely necessary if the married life is to be a good and happy one?

GEOGRAPHY

Tell how the natives of the South Seas use the coconut.

Where is it said always to rain? Give a brief description of the people who live there.

Where can you see oysters growing on trees?

GENERAL KNOWLEDGE

What are the dangers of smelting coal as a ship's cargo?

Give two proverbs on each of the following—lying, anger, sloth, slandering, foolish gossip.

What proverb encourages a girl to keep herself neat, tidy and well clothed?

In what way is Buddhism a good preparation for Christianity?

Describe the feelings of Robert Burns when he (1) found a field mouse (2) saw a daisy.

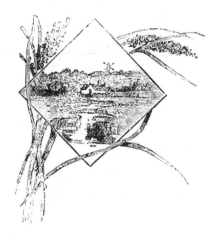

Rewards for the Diligent

We have brought to the girl in the kitchen or at the factory some questions in order to help her to keep up her education and to draw out the powers of her mind.

Occupation is the necessary basis of all honourable enjoyment.

Nothing, not even the studies encouraged by the excellent Association, should be allowed for a moment to come between you and the punctual and faithful discharge of your duties in the home. You are under a Divine Call while occupying the position of Servants to do the good Servant's work to the best of your abilities.

'I liked the questions very much and am very proud to have been given a pen-holder as a prize. The Bible questions seemed very hard but when I saw the answers they were very simple.'

'I found the History questions more difficult although I think they were very good for us as we had to try and express more of what we thought in our own words. I find Macaulay's *History of England* very enjoyable.'

Now the evenings of study by the kitchen fireside are over for a while and when the long summer nights are come and your work is over you will have time for more general reading. But be careful what books you read. Read only those that will help you to live a nobler life and not those which will make you discontented with your lot.

'We working people have nothing in common with the Lords and Ladies that are written about in common books and unless one has something in common with the hero or the heroine of a story I don't think there is much enjoyment or profit in reading it. My favourite author is Annie S. Swan. I like her books because she shows good from evil so clearly.'

The words of a friend who has read and judged many hundreds of your papers on History and Geography still ring in my ears: 'What splendid Wives and Mothers these girls will make!'

Annie Maclaren has in nine years of study received forty-two Prizes and seven Certificates as well as a Prize for four years continuous service in the one place and one for six years continuous service in the same place.

The following are the Prizes which have been selected this year:

1st—A bound volume of *English Illustrated Magazine*
2nd—Macaulay's *Essays*
3rd—*Steps Upward* by Mrs Barnet
Needlework—framed photograph of the President, Lady Aberdeen
Drawing—framed photograph of the German Emperor

We have also awarded 256 Brooches, crossed flags enamelled as Union Jack and Royal Standard.

Success is delightful. Still, after all, it is not everything and many girls have tried and failed. To such I would say, 'Don't be dismayed: trying is good: trying again after failure is better: but trying and trying and trying again is best of all.'

What to do with the Bitties

Broken bread pudding

This pudding will use up the crusts and remnants of bread to be found in every household. All will suit if clean and not mouldy. Gather all into a large bowl, and throw over it as much sweetened milk as the bread is likely to absorb, with two or three tablespoonfuls of finely-chopped suet, and a little salt. Cover until well soaked, then beat the whole smooth, and add two or three well-beaten eggs, a few currants and raisins, and some grated nutmeg. Bake in an ordinary pudding-dish for about an hour-and-a-half.

Beef toast

Take scraps of cold roast beef and mince as finely as possible. Add pepper and salt to taste, and put the mince into a stewpan with a little good gravy. Thicken it with a small piece of butter rolled in flour. Fry the bread, and spread the mince nicely and evenly over it. The addition of a little made mustard is liked by some, in which case spread it on the bread.

To use up potatoes and rice

Take equal quantities of cold rice and mashed potatoes. Season to taste and mix thoroughly. Roll into good sized balls and dip in beaten egg. Dust lightly with breadcrumbs and place in the oven till a golden brown colour. Children love these balls: they look so pretty and are very nice.

Bacon dumpling

Scald and wring $\frac{1}{4}$ lb stale bread, mix with 1 lb flour and bits of bacon chopped fine. Boil three hours in a cloth with room to swell. The more bacon you use the tastier the dish but only a little need be used.

Chicken toast

Remove the bones from the remains of a roast or boiled chicken; pound the meat in a mortar with pepper, salt, and some parsley, which has been par-boiled, and then chopped finely. Add to it one egg well beaten. Put the mixture into a saucepan with a little milk and a knob of butter. Fry the bread and spread the chicken on it.

Precepts for Puzzled Parents

God could hardly put a higher honour on man or woman than to make them Parents of children. Yes indeed, Parents can do anything with their children and bring them up to anything. You may have them grow up well-to-do, looked up to and beloved, or poor wretches whose very rags and crusts come to them in dishonest ways. Parents! See to it! Yours will be the praise or the blame in this world and the next!

The rudiments of good behaviour have to be chiefly negative at the outset—like 'Punch's advice to those about to be married—Don't!'

We are a Nation of grumblers, but the race of grumblers would soon die out if all children were so trained that never did they utter a complaint without being reminded that it was foolish and disagreeable. How easy for a Mother to do this! 'Oh dear! I wish it had not rained today! It is too bad!' 'You do not really mean what you say, my darling. Is it not of much more consequence that the grass should grow than that you should go out to play?'

A very careless Mother who had neglected the spiritual care of her children was called to the death-bed of her eldest daughter. 'Ah, Mother!' cried the child, 'You have taught me how to live, but you have not taught me how to die!'

The distress which you display on your countenance whenever your child utters an evil word or acts unkindly will have its reward in later life.

The Father who raises his hat to his daughter, who steps back and allows the little one to enter the room first because she is a lady, does more to cultivate a ladylike manner than all the books about etiquette that have ever been written.

Every day and many times a day a child should decide for himself points involving pros and cons—substantial ones too. Let him even decide unwisely and take the consequences: that too is good for him. No amount of exhortation can give such an idea of right and wrong as a month in prison.

A single act of selfishness by a Parent can blight the prospects of a young life. A man who had not risen in the world as high as his talents and appreciation merited told me of the moment of shame in his childhood which had drained him of all self-confidence. It was when he had to step up barefoot onto the platform to receive his prize because his father had sold his boots in order to buy liquor.

A Reader tells me: 'I remember the day my Mother taught me the difference between right and wrong. We were in a garden where there were red daisies. She said, "These are Mrs Sommers' daisies: you must not touch them." That is over fifty years ago and I appreciate the moral lesson in it more now than I did then. I was barely two years old but have never forgotten Mrs Sommers' daisies.'

The boy's parents had never taught him to do as he was bid. He had, therefore, no determination, no power to stick to anything good. He never got good work and good wages, and so he drifted from bad to worse. Finally, after years of shame and crime, he stood at the foot of the gallows. He begged leave to speak to his Mother and whispered in her ear, 'It's you have brought me to this! Take this for your pains!' And his last act was to bite off his Mother's ear!

Chicks Own Corner

My dear Chicks,

It would never do for the 'Onward and Upward' Magazine not to have a special corner for you, so we shall reserve a snug place for you from time to time when we have space for it. We should like any stories from you; perhaps you have some pets that you can tell us about.

Your affectionate friend,
Lady Marjorie Gordon

Dear Lady Marjorie,

I had a pet swan and we had it on the lake. But when the ice came it did not like it and it flew up to the farm. Father took me to the farm to ask if they had seen it and we were surprised to see it going to be cooked and all plucked. They thought it was a wild goose.

Nora Constance, Auchterlony

My dear Chicks,

Mother and I have got a very nice plan that I am sure you will all like. This is to have a wee baby magazine inside the big one on purpose for the children.

We beg our readers' special attention to the miniature magazine 'Wee Willie Winkie' which will be published with every issue of 'Onward and Upward'. Mothers should welcome the wee bairn which will always now accompany its elder sister. Sometimes it is difficult to know how to amuse young people and yet it is most important that the home fireside should be made as attractive as possible if it is to hold its own against outside allurements and attractions.

My dear Chicks,

　　　　　Father has bought a pair of black horses whose names are Dick and Bill, and if you pat them and say 'Dick, poor Dick' or 'Bill, poor Bill' they put out their tongues as a sign of satisfaction. We have a pair of Italian horses too which rear up on their hind legs if you say 'Garibaldi'.

Your affectionate friend,
Lady Marjorie Gordon

Dear Lady Marjorie Gordon,

　　　　　My Father has a horse too. He is for his van and is a big brown horse called 'Daftie'. He is such a queer funny horse that he has been called that name.

Competition: What do you do with your pocket money?

Since January my expenditure amounted to one pound and eightpence, but this includes a pair of skates, two books, a bottle of perfume, a fan, a pair of scissors, a pair of party pumps, ice-cream, sweets and lemonade.

Agnes Phair

My dear Chicks,

　　　　　Wee Willie Winkie sighs sadly when he thinks of the number of broken toys which he has seen lying about when he peeped in at various doors and windows which might have been sent for the broken toys competition.

Competition: Write a short story made funny by bad spelling which we can after give to the other bairns as a competition to correct.

What should I tell my Daughter?

That her own room is her nest and that to have it sweet and attractive at all times is a duty as well as a pleasure.

That when God made her body He intended it should be clothed properly and modestly.

That the man who wishes to marry her is the one who tells her so in plain terms and not the one who pours silly love speeches into her ear.

That she should avoid all men who speak lightly of the Great Duties of life.

That her best confidant is her Mother and that nobody sympathises with her pleasures and joys as you do.

That she must think well before she says yes or no but to mean it when she does.

A TINY SERMON

Do not say one word or entertain one thought that you cannot repeat to your Mother, nor do anything which, when the golden day comes you cannot tell to your sweetheart.

MORE ADVICE FROM A MINISTER

Before I marry any young couple I tell them—'Now tomorrow, if you're still of the same mind, I am going to tie the knot. And if I could louse the knot as easily as I can tie it I'd be the thrangest man between Beersheba and Ardnamurchan Point. Think about that before tomorrow.'

Wee Willie Winkie's Puzzle Box

Why is oak the worst kind of wood with which to make a wooden leg?—Because it produces a-corn.

What instrument of the male toilet would suggest itself to the mind of a gentleman when he sees a lady fall?—Razor.

When do two and two not make four?—When they signify twenty-two.

When is a clock like a lazy workman?—When it strikes.

In three degrees of comparison, why does a lawyer go into business, stay in business, and get out of business?—To get on, to get honour, to get honest.

What man sits before the Queen with his hat on?—Her coachman.

Why is love like taking soup with a fork?—You can never get enough of it.

Why are old apples like unmarried ladies?—Because they are often shrivelled and difficult to pare.

When are carpenters like circumstances?—When they alter cases.

When does a lady resemble a nut?—When she has filbert nails, hazel eyes, chestnut hair and a colonel for a husband.

Why was Joseph put in the pit?—Because the boxes and galleries were full.

Every Boy is Somebody's Darling

There's the witty boy and the pretty boy,
  And the boy that oils his hair;
There's the cat-faced boy, and the rat-faced boy,
  And the boy with the bovine stare.

There's the steamy boy and the dreamy boy,
  And the boy who is 'up-to-date';
There's the boy who smokes, and the boy who jokes,
  And the boy who is always late.

The training of a child is a grave responsibility, but when the child is a boy the responsibility weighs most heavily on a Mother's heart.

Let his morning breakfast be porridge. Do you think that a Carlyle, a Livingstone, a Burns could have been produced on wishy-washy tea and bread with shop jam?

We must train our boys to be good soldiers, to be manly, pure and courageous and to be content to be in the position in which they are unless they can come by their own frugality, energy and industry to lift themselves to a higher position.

This is the age of scamped work. Married Associates should train their sons from the outset to be thorough in all they undertake and to practise tasks until they can do them perfectly 'just like Mother or Father always do'.

Many boys have their tempers spoiled and their views of their own powers stunted by the badgering of their sisters.

Many a rough-seeming boy has heart-aches and troubles hidden away under all that careless light-heartedness.

> There's the tender boy and the slender boy,
> And the boy with limbs like a bear's;
> There's the stoutish boy and the loutish boy,
> And the boy who slides downstairs.
>
> There's the cheerful boy and the fearful boy,
> And the boy who deserves a flogging;
> There's the boy with a heart, and the boy too smart,
> And the boy whose brain wants jogging.
>
> There are many others, oh, men and brothers,
> And none are all bad, you bet;
> There are boys and boys, yet through griefs and joys,
> They are somebody's darlings yet.

How Families Get Broken Up

While visiting an Edinburgh orphanage, we came upon a sad example of what happens when Parents neglect their Duties. I asked a poor wee laddie—

'And where is your Father?'
'Faither's in Perth jile'
'Poor fellow', I replied, 'And where's your Mother?'
'Mither's deid', he answered, without a trace of emotion, 'That's why Faither's in Perth jile'.

How A Boy 'Stood By His Gun' To The Last

He was selling papers in a busy thoroughfare. 'Papers! Times, Ledger, Record!' he cried. But the last word was cut short and to my horror I saw his bright face looking upward from beneath the hooves of a team of spirited horses. As I tenderly raised the slight form his eyes fluttered open and he whispered 'Papers, mister. Times, Ledger. . . .' But the neck stiffened, the eyes closed and his head fell heavily against my shoulder.

A Word to the Sons and Daughters who read Onward and Upward

We are getting so advanced nowadays that boys and girls think it altogether beneath their dignity to show courtesy and consideration either for age or authority.

Don't
—be late for meals. Unpunctuality is the greatest cause of domestic disturbance.
—evince any unseemly desire to partake of the most appetising dishes.
—find fault with the fare provided. Think of the hundreds of starving people who have not even a dry crust of bread to eat.

Do
—trust your Mother. You will never have a friend who has your good so much at heart. She is older and therefore wiser than you.
—follow your Parents' advice about the choice of clothes, friends, books and occupations.
—reverence your Mother. She may have foibles about which gentle loving little family jokes may be allowed: do not make too free.

I love the word Tidy: I think it is connected with 'tide', giving the idea of the sea being 'tied' to the sun and so obediently following its attraction. So tidiness is 'tiedness' and gives the picture of one whose whole life is tied up in neat little bundles.

Emulate

—Elsie Anderson who writes, 'I have been saving up my pennies and have managed to buy enough wool to knit bright and cosy cuffs for my father and mother, five sisters and nine brothers and I am busy knitting to have them all ready by Christmas.'

—the children of the Mother who writes, 'My girls leave me nothing to do in the way of housework and sewing. The boys are always inventing something for my comfort—a screen to shade my eyes from the fire, a box for my knitting. Not only my commands but also my wishes are remembered and obeyed: the boys know that I do not like dirty boots in the sitting room: the girls that I cannot bear to see them sitting without something to do with their fingers.'

A SISTER'S LOVE

I cannot think of a more beautiful sight than the affection of a sister for her brother. A sister's love is one of the sweetest flowers planted by God in the heart of a girl. Powerful as is the influence of a mother, there have been innumerable cases where a sister's sweet and tender love has been the saving grace of a brother's life. The sister's conduct in the house often formulates the brother's estimate of her sex. She can have a softening influence on him when all else fails. In fact, a young man can be made pretty well what his sister chooses to make of him. She can coax and train him in those little acts of courtesy due to her sex as nobody else can. Sisterly affection is a softer rod by which to rule than any other measure.

A loving and considerate brother is almost certain to make a good husband. This influence every sister has in her power. She should have the same regard for the neatness of her dress at the breakfast table before her brother as she has at dinner before the brother of some other girl. She should be as kind and polite in her conversation to him as she is to the friend he may bring home with him. 'Tell me what kind of sister she is and I will tell you what kind of wife she will be', is a common saying among men. And often a girl will think, 'He will make a good husband because he has a kind and loving sister.'

Thrifty Ways for Thoughtful Wives

It is a truer kindness to help people to make the best of the little they have than to give them more (*Her Day of Service*)

Save old toothbrushes for cleaning the corners of window sashes.

Worms in furniture may be destroyed by inserting a knitting needle dipped in paraffin in the largest holes every day for a month.

Equal quantities of salt and flour mixed with vinegar makes a good polish for brass.

To prevent grass growing in a yard pour boiling water over the stones whenever the grass shows itself.

Coal ashes mixed with salt and water makes a good cement with which to fill up cracks in many materials.

To catch mice lay fly paper before the holes. When captured they can be destroyed. If care is taken the same paper can be used over and over again.

To kill rats—pounded glass mixed with flour into a paste should be placed near the rat-holes.

Dry pieces of orange peel in the oven after cooking: they make good kindling for the fire.

When darning table-linen use the ravelled threads from old linen articles.

Delicious Drinks for Drowsy Days

Barberry water:

Squeeze the juice of four lemons and two oranges, rub off the rind of two of the lemons on lumps of sugar; put into this a pound of castor sugar and a half pint of water, and enough barberry syrup to flavour, made as follows: One pound of good lump sugar and a pint of water, put this into a preserving-pan and let it boil gently for half-an-hour. Be very careful to remove the scum as it rises, then put in a half a pound of ripe barberries and boil for a quarter of an hour. Strain, and when cold put it in bottles.

Currant water:

Bruise a quart of red currants and half a pint of raspberries. Add half a pound of loaf sugar and two quarts of nice spring water. Put all into preserving pan, and when it begins to simmer have ready three sheets of white glazed writing-paper soaked in water till it has become quite a pulp, and put in; let it stand for a minute or so, and then strain through fine muslin. You may add as much sugar as is agreeable to the taste when taking it.

Rhubarb water:

Take one pound of nice young rhubarb, and cut it in small pieces; put it in a saucepan (an enamelled one if possible) with the rind of a lemon cut very thin and half a pound of lump sugar. Let it boil for half-an-hour, just giving it a stir every now and again, then strain through a jelly bag, or fine muslin, and put it in bottles.

Lemonade:

To a quart of boiling water add the juice of six lemons, and the rind, very finely cut, of one, and a quarter of a pound of castor sugar. Stir all well together, and when cold strain through a jelly bag or very fine muslin, then put it in dry bottles and cork closely. Keep it in as cool a place as possible.

Apricot cordial:

A very nice cooling drink can be made by peeling about one dozen nice ripe apricots, take out the stones, pour on them one quart of boiling water and six ounces of castor sugar. Let it stand for two hours, and then strain through very fine muslin.

Bring Joy and Comfort to your Home

The Home with its fireside and nursery and kitchen, the training of the young and the tending of the sick, is a woman's natural and rightful sphere.

⊷⊱═⊰⊷⊱═⊰⊷

No woman is ready to marry until she has mastered the fine arts of housekeeping. Home is the wife's kingdom. She holds in her hands the happiness of the hearts that nestle there.

⊷⊱═⊰⊷⊱═⊰⊷

In the pages of this Magazine we want to refresh those that are weary and worn with household toil. We will use bright stories, tender words and suggestions of new ways of making the home bright and attractive and the centre of all that is for true happiness and righteousness.

⊷⊱═⊰⊷⊱═⊰⊷

Don't have every corner of your home turned topsy-turvy at Spring cleaning time. Arrange your work so that there shall always be one cosy corner where your Husband can have his paper and his pipe in peace.

⊷⊱═⊰⊷⊱═⊰⊷

Good husbands cannot be spoiled by petting. Bad ones will not be made worse and may be made better. One and all they like it. Not only fondling and love words, but to have their homecomings at evening accounted events. They enjoy pretty surprises and favourite dishes, the flower laid by the plate, the becoming gown or ribbon. It is the 'little by little' that makes up the weal or the woe of married life.

> Govern your temper, much depends on this
> Without it there is not domestic bliss
> An angry word will often stir up strife
> And mar the comfort of a married life.

At meal times, don't discuss the pros and cons of vexed questions. Talking over such things at table has been the ruin of many a good digestion.

⊷⊱═⊰⊷⊱═⊰⊷

A few pieces of charcoal thrown into the pot in which cabbage is being cooked will prevent the unpleasant odour which pervades so many otherwise happy homes.

43

There is a household fiend with a long memory for dates and details. A dozen times a day exasperating frictions are caused by needless corrections referring to matters where exactness is not really imperative.

If the blankets on the bed are too thin to keep the bairnies warm try a large sheet of brown paper or the thickest newspaper you can get and put it just underneath the counterpane. Tuck it tightly all round and you will soon find that the little ones are more comfortable than before.

Home sweet home—a sacred spot—is not what it used to be, a mighty power in the nation. We must try to keep up its strong true influence however. We dare not let it be swept away by the love of excitement and variety so prevalent nowadays.

Make kites for your boys or help them to make them for themselves. Get Father interested in the balancing and flying. Don't grudge to have the litter on the kitchen floor.

Home is man's resting-place. It is woman's workshop and battlefield.

Half a teaspoonful of sugar will usually revive a dying fire.

A Few Suggestions for the Management of Young Children

Oh! If the world would only stop long enough for one generation of Mothers to be properly instructed, what a millennium would begin in thirty years!

Train your first child with special care. When others follow the influence will be great and you will be saved much trouble.

The less rocking, tossing, patting, combing, coaxing, teasing and promiscuous kissing an infant is obliged to endure the better for his health and good nature.

Improper Feeding:

It is wrong to give an infant arrowroot, soaked bread or any other food than milk. No baby every sucked boiled bread from its mother's breast.

Milk is the food that the Creator intends a baby to have and any substitute for it should be looked on as an evil.

Do not offer Nature's fount every time the baby cries. A full stomach is doubtless the cause of its pain.

45

There is no limit to the indiscretion of the East End Mother. She regards beefsteak and gin as suitable nourishment to a year old baby. The appearance of four teeth shows that Nature intends the child to begin biting food.

Cold baths should not as a rule be given to infants until they are a year old.

You cannot begin to sow the seeds of moral education too early. Before it is many weeks old a baby may begin to learn obedience and self-command.

Children should be taught to walk from the first in an upright position with the head up and the chest well thrown out.

Children should be trained to walk alone for they are often made high-shouldered through being led by the hand.

When passion rages calmness and tact may find the cure. A drink of water or some small duty to be done may restore self possession.

The infliction of bodily pain will on some occasions be necessary, but a child must be guarded from the sight of anger as from poison.

The machinery of a child's brain is tender. Do not over-work or over-excite it. Do not interrupt a child when he is making his own observations.

Innocence is a shield against evil, but ignorance may lead to surprise in sin. Teach your child some of the simple facts of plant and insect life and you will easily and naturally enlighten his mind on some of the mysteries of human existence.

Cheerfulness — the Daughter of Employment

A true 'Onward and Upward' housemaid keeps her odd corners, her brasses, her windows as clean as a new pin.

And so, as a Mother loves her child you must learn to love any work you have got to do. Only in this way will you find happiness in your work.

If a stove is blackleaded whilst it is still hot it burns on and will not take the required polish.

It is a high and dignified thing to be a servant. We want our girls to realise that it is a position of great dignity and honour, for which they must use their best powers; that they must put their best thoughts in all the common things of life if they are to be good, trained servants.

> Do what you can, being what you are
> Shine like a glow-worm if you cannot be a star.
> Work like a pulley if you cannot be a crane
> Be a wheel-greaser if you cannot drive the train.

Do not despise your situation. In it you must act, suffer and conquer. From every point on earth we are all the same distance from Heaven.

Garbage cans should be filled with strong boiling soda water twice a week and scrubbed round well with a whisk.

Pray that you may not be ensnared with any lower ambition, either of fortune or leisure or travel, but make it your constant delight to pound away at your daily work, doing all the good you can just where you are.

Sprinkle powdered borax in the kitchen to kill cockroaches.

The opportunities for saving, the contact with educated minds, the superior conditions of life in a refined house are all in favour of domestic service as the best occupation for working girls.

47

Servants have so much in their power, so much of the comfort and well-being of a home lies with them that I confess I think it strange that they do not take a greater pride in exercising the power of good.

Your work is yours alone. Hold it as something sacred: do the meanest thing in a royal way.

When our servants have been working hard to please us they have given us something of more value than can be expressed in pounds, shillings and pence. Let us give them the pride and satisfaction of hearing 'Well done thou good and faithful servant'. This is one of the ways in which we can serve those who serve us.

When sweeping a dusty room scatter damp sawdust or tea leaves all over before commencing operations.

Many girls nowadays go to their first place with one golden rule: 'Don't let yourself be put upon.' Yet in no other trade is the pupil boarded, lodged and paid for learning. The discontents forever changing their situations must be considered as belonging to the ranks of rebellious daughters.

The Onward and Upward Association offers a Prize to every female servant who shall remain in her situation for three years and another, more valuable, Prize for six years.

For Three Years.

For Six Years.

For Ten Years.

Upstairs to Downstairs –
Advice to a Young Servant Girl

How To Make Do On Your Wages

If you write home once a fortnight and visit home once a year that will be quite often enough.

❈

Get a black dress for Sunday, wear it a year then take it for a second best one for when there is company or when it is your Mistress' day 'At Home'. Next year wear it for every day and when it is done use it as an underskirt or send it home for your Mother or Sisters to make use of.

❈

You won't need so many pairs of boots if you wear the old ones in the morning to do the grates: half an hour's kneeling does more harm to a good pair of boots than a week's walking.

❈

It is a bad plan to have your wages paid monthly because you will spend them: ask your Mistress to pay you at the end of six month periods.

❈

Wear yellow cotton underclothes: it lasts much better than white.

❈

Look forward to the time when you will have high wages. You will be able to dress better on Sundays.

❈

If a person commences saving 2d a week at 14 years of age; 6d a week at 18; 9d a week at 20; 1s 0d a week at 24; 1s 6d a week at 27; how much will she have saved at the age of 60? (General knowledge question paper).

❈

Be A Sunbeam In The Kitchen

Keep yourself cheerful to yourself and companionable to your fellow-servants—all of whom will be older than you—by keeping yourself pleasantly and usefully occupied during your leisure hours.

Knit or sew something for your Mother. How pleased she will be to think that you have not forgotten her, and, even amid her pleasure, she may shed a few tears as she wonders whether her lassie still remembers and acts upon advice she has been given.

To knit cuffs for your brothers and sisters may help you for the time being to turn a deaf ear to the, perhaps, not too innocent jokes that are, alas! too predominant in many a kitchen.

If coarse language is being spoken in the kitchen of an evening you might introduce some higher topic which does not lend itself to coarse language. What better way than to ask their help with your Onward and Upward questions? This month's question about the breathing apparatus of the fallow deer might start a good discussion about the wonders of Nature.

We could do much by being as salt in a single conversation, making it wholesome and healthy, by letting in fresh air or by shutting some valve of impurity, or by inspiring enthusiasm in a righteous cause. Let us be women of enterprise!

Be a sunbeam in the kitchen. Perhaps you can sing. It is wonderful what effect a good old Scotch song can produce. In general servants are fond of singing and often will abandon their own idle and coarse talk to listen to a song when no amount of preaching could make them do so. As they sit and listen one fellow perhaps remembers that that song was a favourite of his Mother's. It brings back recollections of her and of the long-forgotten lessons he learned at her knee.

If you have tact enough you might manage to get the other servants to listen to your reading. You might begin with pieces from the *People's Journal* and gradually move on to more serious and profitable reading, perhaps something by Sir Walter Scott or an interesting biography.

PERILS OF THE LEISURE HOURS

A servant girl does not have much leisure time, but it would be better that she had none at all than that she had a great deal and misspent it.

If evil is to be kept out of the hands and the mind something good must keep its place.

Honour and happiness cannot be distilled out of the baser pleasures of life.

She who has no mind to trade with the Devil should keep out of his shop.

> Pussy at the window sits
> Watching every bird that flits
> On the ground to catch the crumbs,
> Keenly eyes it as it comes.
> Yet the birds may safely pass
> Pussy—looking through the glass.
>
> May I as serenely see
> Pleasures never meant for me
> And as readily submit
> To the bounds that God sees fit.
> To confine my wayward will
> As poor Pussy—watching still.

The friendships of the world are often simply confederacies in vice or leagues for the attainment of pleasure.

In most Workhouses most of the unfortunate children are the children of domestic servants. Such things cannot be spoken of, yet they are facts. Girls are given the evening out or the Sunday out and never asked where they have been.

The President of the Onward and Upward Association will give a set of Clothes or an infant Cot to the first child of every Associate who marries respectably.

A Prize will be awarded to the Associate who writes the best essay on the subject 'Virtue is its own Reward'.

In my Lady's Chamber

A lady's maid must feel a thrill of horror at the idea of her Mistress going out with a button off a glove or a stitch out of her gown.

White articles if but slightly soiled are readily cleansed by rubbing with dry flour and hanging out of doors.

Feather beds should be placed in the shade to air, but never set in the sun for it draws out oil and gives the feathers an unpleasant smell.

The bedstead should be washed occasionally with alum and water.

Rosepetals dried and placed in a pretty bowl will give fragrance to the air of a Lady's bedroom.

To rid the bedroom of flies, place a plateful of this mixture on the window-sill:—one teaspoonful of brown sugar, ditto black pepper, with a little cream.

Wilted roses will regain their freshness if dipped a moment or two in hot water.

When providing hot water for the toilet provide also a saucer of precipitated chalk which is the best powder for cleaning teeth without impairing them.

Add a small quantity of alum or ammonia to the footbath to prevent the feet from glowing.

To keep the hair in curl damp it with strong tea in which four large lumps of sugar have been dissolved.

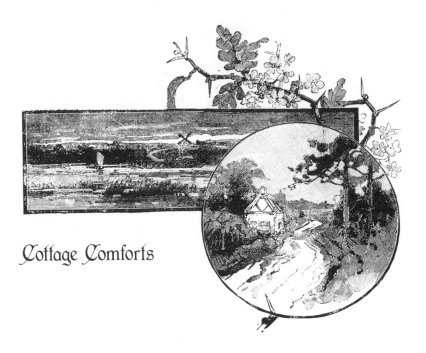

Cottage Comforts

When cooking an old fowl boil it for four hours in water to which bicarbonate of soda has been added.

Ox-cheek soup

First clean a whole ox-cheek carefully with warm water; then soak it for twelve hours in two gallons of cold water; then stew for six hours; strain off the liquor. Next day stew again with some of the liquor, from four to six hours; skim it well. Add pepper, salt, celery, onions, carrots, parsnips. Let all boil gently for four hours; then remove the meat from the bone, cut the meat into pieces, put it back into the soup, and thicken with a little flour mixed smoothly with cold water and poured into the soup, which should be allowed to boil for a quarter of an hour longer. Half-boiled potatoes or cabbage may be added when the meat is again put into the soup.

Herring pancakes

Skin, bone, and cut up a couple of dried herrings, make a light batter of flour, eggs, and milk, drop in the pieces of herring, and fry in boiling butter sufficient of the mixture to form a thick pancake.

Carrot soup

Peel and slice 2 lb carrots and a few onions. Fry in a saucepan. Add 2 quarts stock, pepper and salt. When the vegetables are tender, take them out and pulp them through a sieve. Add as much of the stock as will give the thickness required. Bring to the boil and add sippets of toast in the tureen.

A dish for a family of children

Take a quarter of a pound of lean bacon, and cut it up in pieces, put it into a large saucepan or pot with one pound of whole rice, three onions cut in slices, a little parsley, and a few peppercorns. Cover them with three pints of water, and boil slowly. When it is done put the pot by the side of the fire, the rice will swell, and take up the water, and remember that as rice requires a great deal of room to swell, allowance should be made at first for it in choosing a large saucepan or pot.

Common nettles

Well wash a pailful of nettles. By grasping them very firmly in the hand you will find that they do not sting. Have a good sized pan half full of boiling water. Add a piece of washing soda about the size of a bean, a handful of salt and the nettles. Boil for $\frac{1}{4}$-hour and drain free of water. Lightly chop and put back in the pan with dripping and serve with butter. The nettles are best in the early Spring.

Rosemarkie, N.B.

Open Your Alabaster Boxes now

You have not fulfilled every duty unless you have fulfilled that of being cheerful, pleasant, and helpful to others.

Seize every opportunity to be useful as eagerly as if your life depended on it: somebody else's life may, and yours will be made the richer.

> Do the work that's nearest
> Though it's dull at whiles
> Helping when you meet them
> Lame folk over stiles.

Do not keep the Alabaster Boxes of your love and tenderness until your friends are dead. Open them now. Fill their lives with sweetness. Speak approving cheering words while their ears can hear them and while their hearts can be thrilled by them. The kind things you mean to say when they are gone, say before they go. The flowers you mean to strew on their coffins, send them now to brighten their homes before they leave them. I would rather have a plain coffin without a flower than a life without the sweetness of love and sympathy.

'Stay at home', said Inclination
'Let that mercy visit wait'
'Go at once!' said Duty sternly
'Or you'll be too late.'

You will smile if now I tell you
That this quiet strife,
Duty conquering Inclination
Strengthened all her life.

TWO LOVELY STORIES

Noticing how excited the little kitchen maid was at the sight of the busy
city street, her Mistress proposed to take the girl to a restaurant and to
give her whatever she might choose from the bill of fare, while she called
for pen and paper and wrote her business letter. Polly modestly chose a
glass of milk and a bun, but she could hardly eat for excitement while
her eager eyes feasted on the novel scene around her.

'Oh Miss!' she exclaimed as they were leaving, 'I have never known
what it is to be happy before today!'
Her Mistress choked back a sob of emotion and called for a cab.

There is no limit to the good you can exercise as an individual. I often
recall the story of the little girl who was converted by reading a
sixpenny New Testament found by her on the pavement and who did
what she could by laying aside a penny every day with which, on the
Saturday, she bought another New Testament and presented it to one of
her fellow workers in the mill. And so the leaven spread until there was
not a mill in the town where there was less swearing and coarse
language and quarrels about wages and work.

Comfort for Weary Mothers

Childish arms about thee twining
Cheeks to thine most fondly prest
Happy laughter in the gloaming
Could ye be more sweetly blest?

'Dear Lady Aberdeen. I am afraid that you will think me very presumptuous in writing to you, but I think I would be helping others as well as myself if I suggested that you set aside a page for advice to working men's wives. I do long to train my children but if you could understand how tired and weary one gets with no help and not very strong.'

Every Mother has her dark days—when the little voices sound so shrill and piercing and the little tempers unruly. Do not be downcast: generally speaking this is the result of the Mother's physical weariness and if possible she should take a rest for an hour or two.

Try a change of occupation. If you are weary with wielding a hot iron some darning and mending can be as welcome as a rest.

Impatient, angry tones never did any good. For your own sake as well as the children's, learn to speak low. They will remember that tone when your head is under the willows. So too will they remember a harsh and angry voice. Which legacy will you leave to your children?

The waywardness and freaks of unamiable disposition in her children produce petulance and irritability and perhaps lead often to unseemly anger. A scolding, a slap, or a shake sometimes takes the place of firm but mild expostulation and calm correction. To Mothers who are tempted to this course of action I say—What you need and what you must win by contrast and determined effort is the complete subjugation of your own temper.

O Mother dear the tide may roll
The rooted lily will not move
And time can never change the soul
That's anchored in a Mother's love.
(From 'Mother's Love' by Fanny Buckley-Owen)

Some Mothers, sadly, fail to realise the immense responsibility and privilege of motherhood, forgetting that to the Mother is entrusted the care and training of a Being that is immortal, to live on for weal or woe through all eternity.

At our first Onward and Upward Association tea-meeting, one Mother told me that she had very much enjoyed it because she had not been out to tea for over twenty years, for she always had one child in arms to care for.

There is no limit in this country to the rise of the most humbly born of her children to power, wealth and position: so we cannot measure the future influence of our children any more than we can fathom the depth of the ocean.

One good Mother is worth a hundred schoolmasters.

A list of some helpful books for Mothers:

A Bright Sunset—the last days of a Football Player, by his Mother
My Little Corner, by Mrs Walton
Christy's Old Organ, by Herba Stretton
Mothers and Mothers or Hattie's Mistake by Mrs Mayo
Ragged Homes and How to Mend them, by Mrs Bayley
Comfort Cottage, by Mrs Wigley
A Man is what a Woman makes him (Tract Society)
Blessed be Drudgery, by Dr Gannett, BD

Mrs Maud Counter's Folding Ironing Board.

Willie Winkie's Riddle-me-Ree

1. What fashionable game are frogs fond of?
2. When can 'donkey' be spelt with one letter?
3. What is the difference between a steamboat and a flower-girl?
4. When was St Paul a pastry baker?
5. If you saw a policeman on fire what poet's name would you think of?
6. My first a baby does when you smack it
   My second a lady says but does not mean it
   My third needs pegs to fix the washing to it
   My whole contains a girl's best half in it.
7. Where does all the snuff in the world go to?
8. What is the difference between a doctor and a cobbler?
9. When Adam was asked what his religion was what did he say?
10. What is so brittle that if you pronounce its name you break it?
11. Why should a person who hates gambling not travel by the 12.50 train?
12. If a gentleman saw a lady about to fall what famous soldier's name would he call?
13. My first's a useful article
    Of every-day attire
    Whose modern styles and fancies
    One cannot quite admire
    My next's a common colour
    In nature and in art
    My whole an evil passion
    In many a human heart.

Answers:

1 Croquet: 2 When it's U:
3 One stems the tide and the other ties the stems:
4 When he went to Phillipi: 5 Bobby Burns:
6 Crinoline: 7 No one nose:
8 One heals the body and the other heels the sole:
9 He didn't exactly know but he thought Evangelical:
10 Silence: 11 Because it's ten to one he'll catch it:
12 Caesar: 13 Hatred.

FAREWELL TO WEE WILLIE WINKIE

From the Editor's letter in the last issue of *Wee Willie Winkie* (Midsummer, 1897).

Poor deserted bairnies! What can we say to you and what can we do for you? We can at least mingle our tears together over the loss of our little comrade and playmate.

Your farewell letters have touched us. We feel that a real bond of sympathy unites Wee Willie Winkieites all over the world.

Will you make us one promise for auld lang syne? We would like all comrades of Wee Willie Winkie to promise that they will never read a book or paper which they think Wee Willie and his Editors would not like or would think bad or foolish.

> Tell me, oh doting parents
>   Counting your household joys,
> Rich in your sweet home-treasures,
>   Blest in your girls and boys;
> After the school is over,
>   Each little student freed,
> After the fun and frolic,
>   What do the children read?

A Dozen Don'ts for Wise Wives

Don't be oblivious to the fact that it is far easier to win a man's love than to keep it.

Don't be eagerly desirous for the last word in any matrimonial dispute you may have.

Don't be untidy and slovenly in your dress at any time: above all do not appear at the matutinal meal in *déshabillé*.

Don't think it too undignified to give way to your husband on important matters.

Don't tease the good man when he returns home in the evening with trivial domestic anxieties.

Don't neglect any of the little arts and graces that tend to make a home happy, bright and cheerful.

Don't act as if you thought your relatives superior to his: make much of them, especially his Mother.

Don't fret to know what the matter is when your husband does not look as pleasant as he might.

Don't allow your husband to meddle with home matters that do not concern him.

Don't overspend the housekeeping money: requests for more money are the most fruitful source of domestic dissension.

Don't pretend to understand what your husband is talking about if you really do not. He will be happy if you ask him to put it into simpler words that you can understand.

No little jealous feelings once indulge
Nor ought entrusted to you ere divulge
Accept your Husband's leadership and show
That you shall honour him in all you do.

A meek and quiet spirit should adorn
Each loving wife and everywhere be worn
No golden crown can be compared to this
It is the secret of domestic bliss.

A HOMILY FOR HUSBANDS:

Bear all her burdens for her.

If you want her to submit to your judgment never ask her to submit to your selfishness.

A woman's life is made up of little things: make her happy by little courtesies.

> All day the wife had been toiling
> From an early hour in the morn
> And her hands and her feet were weary
> With the burdens which she had borne.
> But she said to herself 'The trouble
> That weighs on my mind is this
> That Tom never bothers to give me
> A comforting hug or a kiss.'

Love is a wife's only wages. Don't scrimp on your pay.

Puddings that Save your Pennies

In the cold winter months there's nothing like a good pudding to give the bairnies—and the grown-ups as well—a nice comfy feeling inside.

Broken bread pudding (boiled)
Three quarters of a pound of stale bread soaked and beaten to a pulp, quarter of a pound of suet chopped fine, quarter of a pound of flour. Mix well; tie tightly in a floured cloth and boil for two hours.

Hen's nest pudding
Put four or five (pared and cored whole) apples in a pie-dish and surround with sago and water, put in the oven and bake for an hour or more. The apples will rise to the top. This is a most wholesome and economical pudding, and always much liked by the little ones.

Honey-comb pudding
Dissolve nearly an ounce of gelatine in water over the fire. Add one-third of a breakfast-cupful of sugar, and stir till this melts. Beat the yolks of 3 eggs, mix with a breakfast-cupful of milk, and put into the pan with the sugar and gelatine. Stir until the eggs begin to curdle a little, then take off the fire, and, when nearly cold, add the beaten whites of the 3 eggs. Flavour to taste. Put into a mould, and turn out when firm.

Vanilla cream
Soak two-thirds of a sixpenny packet of gelatine in $\frac{1}{2}$ pint of water or milk. Let it stand till the gelatine has absorbed the water, then pour over it $\frac{1}{2}$ pint boiling water or milk, and stir till quite dissolved. Switch up for a few minutes 1 pint of cream, then add 6 ounces of sifted sugar; go on switching till it is light and spongy, then mix in gently the gelatine and 1 teaspoonful of extract of vanilla. Pour into mould.

Gingerbread pudding

Put $\frac{1}{2}$ lb very dry crusts into a very clean linen cloth, and boil them for one minute in water; then wring with all your force, and turn the mass out. Mix with it $\frac{1}{2}$ lb flour, 2 oz suet, $\frac{1}{4}$ lb sugar, $\frac{1}{2}$ oz ground ginger, and $\frac{1}{4}$ oz ground cinnamon. Beat all up and tie quite tight in a cloth, or press into a well-greased shape, and boil it three hours.

Plum pudding

Take $\frac{1}{4}$ lb each of suet, flour and brown sugar, 1 lb of dates (at 2d a lb) and a quarter of a nutmeg grated. Mix all the ingredients, moistening with as little water as possible. Boil for four hours in a buttered basin. Sufficient for six persons at a cost of 5d!

God's Sentinels

Does not Man live by the sweat of his brow—and Woman by the pangs of a loving heart?

> Good women are God's sentinels
> In the darkness of earth's night.
> They hold with stout hearts silently
> Life's outposts towards the light.
> And at the Almighty's Roll Call
> Mong the host that answer 'Here!'
> The voices of good women
> Will sound strong and sweet and clear.

Here surely lies the difference between the service of men and women. Man has to serve those whom he cannot see and does not love. Woman needs something within reach of her hands and heart.

Clean and polish copper kettles by cutting a lemon in two, dipping one of the pieces in salt and rubbing well over the copper.

A great man gains his true influence by eloquent and exciting speeches. A woman gains hers by a thousand silent ministrations.

To get rid of the smell of paint plunge a handful of hay into a pailful of water and let it stand in the newly painted room.

Do your best to be pretty as well as good. A pretty girl has more influence than a plain one—both being equal in other things.

Women long to help and comfort those whom they love. 'Help with your hands', says one of the greatest novelists of the day. Let women claim all such domestic duties that fall to their share: let them watch for them: let them pray for them. Let that woman whose life is most firmly set in the simple lines of daily household duty count herself the happiest of women.

'If she have diligently followed every good work', says St Paul. There is no limit here to what is meant by 'work'. It may be a poor girl's service of cleaning and scouring, a Mother's needlework, a wife's cooking, or a great lady's gift of a picture or an educational endowment. There is good work to be done on every line of life that tends Onward and Upward.

Wash floor tiles with kerosene to make them take on a polish. But remember that the best and most economical polish of all is 'elbow grease'.

"'Remember what your Father used to say.'"

Her Day of Service

By Mrs Isabella Fyvie Mayo, Author of *Equal to the Occasion, At Any Cost*, etc.

CHAPTER I: YOUNG MAN AND MAIDEN

A wild October morning in the North Country. A background of low hills, all bare save one, dark with pine and fir. The express for London is nearly due but there are few people on the windswept platform. One or two sporting gentlemen, an old woman carrying poultry in a basket, another woman in widow's mourning, accompanied by a tall girl and a slim lad also in mourning. It is clear that the girl is going on a long journey.

How much there is to say in those last moments! And how little one does say! The engine comes in sight.

'Margaret! you will be sure to write regularly,' says the widow. 'Remember we are two together here and you are one away by yourself.'

'I am not likely to forget, Mother,' answers the girl. 'Be sure to go home briskly and have a cup of tea. You will have to look after her now, Robert. And now, Mother, good-bye, good-bye.' There is a passionate strength in her clasping arms, but the clear voice is steady and the blue eyes are not dimmed though perhaps a little of the shell-pink brightness has faded from the face, round which the bright hair waves like an aureole.

'Oh Margaret!' sobbed the widow. 'Remember what your dear Father used to say—that life comes to us as we take it and goes with us as we make it.'

'I'll do my very best' answers the girl as she springs lightly into a third class carriage, followed by the old dame with the basket. There is another traveller in the carriage but Margaret does not even see him as she waves her last farewell.

Oh low hills and distant pine-wood, and nearer autumn glories, what is this mist which rises and shuts you out as the train continues its southward race? Margaret raises her hands to her face. But no, she must not break down lest the old neighbour with the poultry returns tomorrow and rends her mother's heart by a recital of how her girl had 'given way'. The other traveller, a young man of vigorous limb, with a Glengarry bonnet pushed up from his broad forehead, seemed to be reading his newspaper, but he knew how the girl was feeling, for he too had said farewell to his native place and the graves of his forefathers.

The old dame regarded Margaret.

'It'll be waesome for your mother without you. I wonder ye did not think of a decent trade for yersel'. It would have been genteeler than being a servant.'

'I chose service,' said Margaret, 'because it will give me the life most like what I would have had in Father's house if he had lived.' Indeed the girl was one of those who looked at domestic service as simply the doing for hire what all women delight to do for love, and doing anything for hire did not mean that it was not done also for love.

'Weel weel' replied the gossip, 'each to his taste. But it's a hard life serving others.'

'Yes' replied the girl with quiet dignity 'but it is good to work hard and to get things out of oneself.' She was quite unconscious that the young man in the Glengarry heard her simple philosophy and took it gladly to his heart, for he was going out to a far land, bare of all but his own strong manhood, and Margaret's chance phrase had for him a significance beyond her meaning—as every word from a pure heart always has. Surely he too had the strength to labour, to fell his own share of the primeval forest and turn the woodland monarchs into beam and rafter and chimney nook. And he would have home-made furniture and wear home-made clothes and would have thoughts of his own and would lay down simple ways of being and doing good without fear of the moth and rust of convention.

'Yes,' he thought, 'it is nice to be able to get things out of oneself.'

Other people entered and left the compartment at intervals, among them a weary looking mother with a child in her arms and another at her side. Margaret took the little child on her knee and relieved the mother by amusing it at the window. She gave up her corner seat to an old lady. She rendered some assistance to an old gentleman who was irritated over a refractory luggage strap. After that he grew chatty and carried on an edifying and diverting conversation with the young man, Margaret going on quietly with her knitting, as unobtrusive as the oil that keeps a machine working smoothly. She gave a spray of rowans to a cripple girl who got in at a big, dirty junction and who looked longingly at them. She gave the best of her sandwiches to the children. And as they drew near their destination she produced a bottle of water and a napkin and refreshed her dusty face. For in her father's cottage she had been trained in habits as dainty as those of a lady. Dirty she might have to be at times, in conflict with dirt, but never in neglect of it. As the train drew into the station the young man handed her out her basket. How he would like to help her further! But their brief acquaintance gave no warrant for such a courtesy. He was not one of those who intrude on friendliness and simplicity. Nor was Margaret one of those who are so intruded upon. A lady approached and introduced herself as Miss Newton, come to meet Margaret and take her to her destination.

'But what a crowd there is round the luggage van!' she exclaimed. The young man offered his services and brought the box marked 'Margaret

Ede'. He explained that he would be continuing his journey, far across the sea.

'Good-bye Sir', said Margaret, 'and a safe arrival.'

'And a prosperous coming back' added Miss Newton. And she saw in his eyes that which made her think, 'If I had a son such as him I should pray that every good woman he met might give him a blessing.'

She said aloud, 'Come along, Margaret, I will put you in a cab that will take you to your mistress's door.'

CHAPTER II: HER MORNING OF SERVICE

ecause of her good upbringing and excellent character references, Margaret Ede had been made a beneficiary of an ancient charity known as Bissett's Bequest, under which orphan girls of respectable birth, whose parents, that is, had fulfilled the rigorous requirement of a high moral code, were given an annual sum of money to purchase their uniforms and working clothes and to help them maintain themselves in bare necessities during the first few years of domestic service. For this reason Margaret was able to enter the service of Mrs Foster, a kindly and well bred lady whose reduced circumstances would not have allowed her to hire a servant had it not been for the charity of the aforementioned Christopher Bissett.

She could not have been more fortunate in her first mistress. Mrs Foster was open with Margaret in all her dealings. She let her see plainly how much—or rather how little—was spent in keeping the household machinery a-going. She showed Margaret how many of the refinements of life are its economies rather than its expenses; that nothing is so extravagant as roughness, hurry or makeshift; and that our bodily necessities are not very exacting if we keep the mind to its proper functions instead of allowing it to pamper our tastes and fancies.

'Good morning Maggie' she said one morning shortly after her new maid had taken up her duties. 'Let me tell you that the cat always gets its food from me, which is the sort of friendly attention that animals appreciate. My view about our duty to animals is that we should give them what is good for them, and nothing good which they cannot appreciate. They do appreciate love, Maggie, but they don't want sentiment. When we give them what only humans can accept and return, we are wasters. And waste is a dreadful thing, Maggie. I think waste is at the bottom of everything terrible that is going on in the world.'

When Margaret came in to clear away the breakfast her mistress watched her as she gathered up the crumbs, glancing as she did so at the trees in the garden.

'Ah! I see I need not remind you to remember the birds' commented the old lady.

'We always did that at home' said Margaret.

'I'm glad' continued Mrs Foster 'that you don't despise the London sparrows for I love them especially because, being saucy thankless quarrelsome songless birds—very like ourselves—we know that God cares for them nevertheless.' Later she came into the kitchen.

'That bowl is for my neighbour Mrs Bates' dinner. I found out that she had to live on scraps of cold meat and cheese as she can do no cooking. I pointed out that these miserable meals cost her above three shillings a week and promised that if she gave me the three shillings a week she could have a nice hot meal of whatever I have. It is a truer kindness to help people make the best of what they have than to give them more. But now Margaret, I should like to explain why I wish your services to me to be as serviceable as they can be to other people also.'

'I'm sure I'm only too glad, ma'am' said Margaret with quickening interest. 'What can anybody want more than to be as useful to as many people as possible?'

'I'm glad you feel it in that light. Still, I should like you to know the exact state of things. You know that it is only because of the Bissett Bequest that you can afford to keep yourself in uniform, outdoor clothing and other personal things. Well, in the same way, I would not be able to afford to keep you in food and lodgings were it not for a good woman who said she would give me enough money every year to maintain a girl, whom I was to train in good ways. It would be our little effort, she said, to train good girls in good ways, to substitute for the household plagues we hear so much about, household missionaries of order and purity and peace. We had earnest consultation over the question of what wage you should have. We decided that although it was quite fair that you should receive board and lodgings, all your other wants should be supplied by parents, friends or benefactions such as the Bequest. We feel that if this were generally done parents and friends would take a more active interest in a servant girl's welfare, and that they would be less likely than they sometimes are to encourage her in the foolish restlessness and insubordination by which girls often damage their own interests and give annoyance to their employers. So we decided not to give you any wages. You can understand, Margaret, how under such circumstances I wish to make this lady's kindness do as much good to other people as I can. There should be no sadder moment in a woman's life than the moment when she has to say "No" to a person in need.'

There was a strange mist in Margaret's eyes. 'I know, ma'am,' she said, 'There was an old man to whom we gave oatmeal every week while father lived, but when he died Mother had to say—'. Margaret choked there. 'I never saw Mother cry as much as then.'

There was silence for a few minutes, then Mrs Foster continued, 'The kind lady who is your benefactress, and mine, is the lady who occupies the apartment above this one, Miss Newton, who met you at the station. She is a very great friend and you will meet her here very often. She is a very busy person, for although she is much occupied with painting pictures she herself keeps no servant.'

Mrs Foster saw the question in Margaret's eyes. 'The reason I am not free to tell you, Margaret; it is a closely held secret. All I can say is that many years ago a sad event happened in her life and she was determined that, as long as strength remained with her, she would do all her own housework as well as continue with her good works and exercise her considerable talent as an artist.'

That afternoon Miss Newton called and greeted Margaret with a quiet smile and a warm handshake. There was assurance and helpfulness in her every trait, kindliness in her beaming eyes, power in her resolute mouth. She was not a young woman, having reached that time of life when, unless soul and character shine through, beauty grows as dim as a stained glass window with no light behind. After Margaret had tidied away the tea-cups her mistress explained some more of the ways in which she and Miss Newton rendered their service. Every piece of blank paper which came into the house was saved. Two little boys, sons of a charwoman, came for them and used them to practise their writing and arithmetic. Miss Newton had complimented Margaret on the fine oatcakes she had baked and volunteered to keep Margaret in an overflowing barrel of oatmeal if she would treat the two little boys to bowls of porridge when they came for the waste paper, and persuade them to take away some oatcakes at cost price.

'What a mistake it is to think that it is dull to be with old people' Margaret told herself. But then all old people are not like Mrs Foster.

CHAPTER III: STRANGERS WITHIN MISS NEWTON'S GATES

s Margaret's acquaintance with Miss Newton developed into friendship, she came to learn more of her ways. The visitors to Miss Newton's apartment were not the type of people whom one meets at morning calls and kettledrums. Some were in rags; many were in mourning. Some came weeping; others crept along the passage and up the stairs by the wall as if they feared that somebody might see them. Others came boldly, even insolently. Miss Newton held that Christian charity had a duty to discharge towards pert young women and saucy mill-girls as well as to those who had slipped further on the downward path. In her good works Miss Newton solicited the willing help of Margaret with increasing frequency and grew to love the silent practical girl who strove to turn every good word she heard into some good work to be done, and who seemed to seek only to know how best to be 'the servant of all'. Margaret was to Miss Newton as a refreshing draught of spring water is to a tired and heated traveller.

At first, Margaret was startled and terrified by the discovery of how near tragedy lies to the commonplace. She felt as if she stood on a narrow brink, with the nethermost gulfs beneath yawning for her, when a man with whose face she had become quite familiar because he kept a shop nearby, and whom she had once seen drive away a dog that threatened to fasten on a kitten, was condemned to death for a brutal murder. She and Miss Newton went with his wretched wife when she visited him in the condemned cell, and waited at the prison gate to receive her in anguish after bidding him the last good-bye. Together they took the woman and her children to Miss Newton's rooms on the terrible night before the ghastly morning. That was a secret between Margaret and Miss Newton. Mrs Foster was to be spared.

There was a different line of vivid interest in life when two rough and bold-eyed factory girls, despairing of getting positions as domestic servants, made up their minds to emigrate to the bush and came every evening to Mrs Foster's kitchen to get initiated by Margaret into common household duties. Margaret went with Miss Newton to see the girls on board the emigrant ship. She could not have dreamed of such a scene—so pathetic and so stimulating. As Miss Newton saw her lip quiver with excitement at the animated scene, she said, 'The world is full of comings and goings. I wonder what has become of the young man in the Glengarry who was so helpful when you travelled to London?' Margaret did not tell Miss Newton that he had been in her mind too at that very moment.

Among her regular work and occasional interest Margaret had not much time for reading. She was not a greedy reader, as few of us are who find plenty to learn from the life around us. Whenever her work in the kitchen allowed her, she availed herself of her mistress' permission and slipped quietly into the parlour to listen to Miss Newton reading a chapter from a book to old Mrs Foster. Margaret always took some knitting or mending, feeling that she was not able to understand enough of what was read to justify idleness. But many a high thought condensed in a melodious sentence dropped upon her mind and stayed there: and many a lofty train of thought which her youth and inexperience made her fail to follow up, yet let down sweetness and strength upon her soul. Only sometimes in the midst of the discourse which followed the readings, Miss Newton grew suddenly silent and Margaret would notice on her face a look which showed plainly enough that she did not see even the fire into which she was gazing. No, she saw something else, some secret from the past, perhaps nowhere in the world at all now. What was it? Margaret could not help the question sometimes. But for any hint she gave, Miss Newton might have lived all her life a grown-up woman, painting her pictures, doing her own housekeeping, in her second-floor flat. Margaret secretly admired Miss Newton's handwriting (and everything else she did) and was inspired with a hope that she might some day rival her penmanship. Will some ladies judge that ambition to be as upsetting as the commoner one of envying her mistress's bonnet?

Almost exactly two years after Margaret entered her service, old Mrs Foster died peacefully in her sleep. It was a terrible blow to poor

Margaret, though she had Miss Newton with whom to take temporary refuge. In her will Mrs Foster left everything unconditionally to Miss Newton.

'My client told me,' said the lawyer, 'that you would know her wishes and would understand how to adapt and modify them with a living love instead of by a rigid dead hand.'

Miss Newton claimed Margaret's help in this matter. The furniture was to be distributed among the aged folk round about. Such pictures as had not been asked for by kinsmen were to go to the Incurable Hospital. Some handsomely bound volumes on theology were to go to the rector and the remainder to the workhouse. Scraps of dainty old china were to be Miss Newton's, and all the dead woman's wearing apparel was to be at the disposal of Margaret for the time being.

After the simple funeral a few friends and relatives returned to Mrs Foster's rooms to share a modest meal which Margaret had prepared. The tea was taken from Mrs Foster's old-fashioned caddy, the jelly jar had her name written on the cover, nay the very candy peel in the cake had been cut by her. There was something very pathetic about the posthumous hospitality. They nearly choked over it and they looked wistfully round the prim pleasant chamber so soon to be dismantled.

'And what is to become of the little servant?' asked one of the gentlemen, having noticed the girl's grieved face. 'Will she enter your service?'

'She will stay with me', replied Miss Newton 'until she finds another situation.'

When they were alone, Miss Newton added, 'You know, Margaret, that for a certain reason I keep no servant. You must come to visit me often, but as a friend. To lose my housework would be a worse blow than to lose whatever little talent I may have as a painter. If you take away my housework you take away my life.'

Then as they stood in the tender sunshine which crept in through the window, and watched the embers dying, for the last time, in Mrs Foster's hearth, Miss Newton lifted up her voice in a wail of bitter weeping. And Margaret knew that although the tears were prompted by the memory of the sweet life just floated away, they also welled out of the secret depths of which she knew nothing. Margaret did not resent the reserve which Miss Newton steadily maintained about the hidden sorrow of her past life. She stole quietly from the room, leaving Miss Newton alone with her secret grief.

CHAPTER IV: 'A SUNBEAM DOWNSTAIRS'

n her search for a new situation Margaret had experience of many domestic interiors. She was kept waiting in one hall because the mistress had not come down stairs at eleven o'clock in the morning. She was offered a position in two homes where several servants were kept and where men in smart liveries opened the door, but Miss Newton was able to inform her that, although the wages were high and the service easy, there was in neither of these homes the love of God nor any righteous household guidance. One evening, after two fruitless interviews, she turned homeward, depressed. Miss Newton had word of a vacancy in a household nearby.

'But I hardly think you will consider it suitable,' she warned. 'Their name is Brunton. There are the husband and wife and two pert and rather unruly children and the husband's young assistant. They keep only one servant, and poor Mrs Brunton is nearly worn out with the trouble the girls have given her. They lie and steal and smash dishes and go off without a moment's notice. And she's in terror lest the children learn more of their bad ways. It would be a thoroughly unpleasant position for the most capable of servants.'

'Is she a nice lady?' asked Margaret eagerly.

'A dear little soul' answered Miss Newton, warmly, 'who would be as bright as a kitten if she got a mite of a chance.'

'I'll go and offer myself', said Margaret.

The interview between Mrs Brunton and her proved highly satisfactory. Margaret felt once more at peace within, self-assured that she had not been guilty of trivial 'picking and choosing' in her quest for a suitable position. Miss Newton went with her and seized the opportunity to have a private talk with Mrs Brunton.

'Margaret is a girl on whom you may rely,' said Miss Newton. 'I want you to feel able to regard her as I am sure you regarded your first servant before a long series of disappointments taught you distrust.'

'Oh Miss Newton,' cried Mrs Brunton. 'What you say is quite true! I started with the determination not to lock things up, and to let the girls have a friend to tea or supper sometimes and to let them have a walk when their work was done. But what came of it? They took the jelly I had made in case of sickness and spread it on their bread and butter, and they took my clothes and wore them. They sold our food to strangers at the back door and they would run out without my leave and sometimes stay out till after ten at night. And when one of them went to trial for stealing, the magistrate said that because I never used keys I had led her into temptation.'

Miss Newton could hardly forbear smiling at the little excited woman, but she knew it was no smiling matter. When one realises the influence such experiences must have on domestic peace it becomes truly tragic.

Margaret's life with the Bruntons was in sharpest contrast with her life with Mrs Foster. Mrs Brunton had started as a married woman about ten years before with the stock of household experience usually possessed by well brought up girls in the lower middle class. She had no natural authority. Her servants were saucy and rebellious from the first with all the extravagant ideas about 'butcher meat' etc. common to the lowest class in great cities. Busily occupied in his chemist shop, Mr Brunton could do little to help. Like many clever young men rising in the world he had been fascinated by the meretricious charms of a lovely but empty headed girl. When her babies came, Mrs Brunton was forced to waive entirely her attempts at household supervision and to tolerate wasteful practices in one girl and undue licence in another. So her domestic ideals sank until she dared aim at nothing higher than the day-to-day securing of a little domestic quiet amid the increasing friction and worry.

As a result the kitchen was in a distressing state of confusion. Margaret set to work with a will. What was the use of knowing how to make war with waste and disorder if one shrank from confronting these enemies in their strongholds? She felt it a wonderful experience to discover that after being so happy with Mrs Foster she could be equally happy in a life absolutely the reverse of the other. In the one she had learned and followed: here she found herself obliged to take the lead. There she had ministered chiefly to feeble old age which had responded with pathetic gratitude; here she was mainly at the service of saucy ungrateful childhood. But Kate and Jem, whom the other servants had regarded as 'plagues' and 'spies' and had only approached with bribery and threats, gradually found contentment as 'Margaret's useful little helpers'. Margaret needed much patience to overcome certain pre-dispositions which her predecessors' bad habits had wrought in the children. She detected Jem in telling a lie, and Mrs Brunton tearfully owned that she and her husband were greatly distressed at the boy's habit of prevarication. Margaret had a long quiet talk with the boy. She told him of a falsehood she herself had uttered when a girl and how the memory of her father's grieved face would sometimes haunt her yet. Her plan for helping him to rid himself of the evil habit was, when she asked him any question which he was likely to hesitate in answering, he would go to his room and think it over for five minutes before he replied. At first he would outstay the five minutes and come back with hanging head and reluctant tongue. But presently he could scarcely have reached the door of his chamber before he came back brightly with a frank recital. And oh how many pleasant maternal theories Mrs Brunton and Margaret were able to put in practice now that the domestic machinery worked regularly without the perpetual terror of breakdowns.

Mrs Brunton regularly heard their lessons. Margaret taught Kate how to knit and let her watch her ironing, and could soon allow her to do all the 'goffering'. As for Jem he was soon able to chop wood and go errands 'like a little gentleman' as Mrs Brunton expressed it. When

autumn came the children had a perfect saturnalia in picking fruit for
jam, and Mrs Brunton herself spent a day in her bright 'new' kitchen,
arrayed in a white apron and felt that she was a girl again, back in her
father's pantry. And Mr Brunton was brought downstairs in triumph to
see the hundred jars all neatly covered and labelled.

'I believe you've got the sweetness out of the jam already' he said,
patting his little wife playfully on the cheek, whose sudden flush of
pleasure recalled to him the bonnie blushes of his courting days.

CHAPTER V: QUINTON RENDALL FINDS THE WAY UPWARD

r Brunton's young assistant, Quinton Rendall was a good looking boy who had never had any true home life and to whom the names father and mother had no endearing or elevating associations. When he heard of the charms of home life he thought of his tired employer with his fretful children on his knee, his wife upstairs with a sick headache, and a sluttish maid bringing in bad coffee and tough toast. Was it for this that he was asked to forgo the 'pleasures' of youth and betake himself to habits of thrift, industry and self restraint? It seemed to him a poor bargain.

And so Quinton Rendall drifted on in life. Nobody ever drifts upwards. It takes all our most strenuous efforts to resist the currents that are always ready to bear us down. Quinton scarcely knew what upward and downward means in any moral sense. Was not such a one the soil in which bad seeds are sure to flourish? By the time Margaret entered the Bruntons' service Quinton had a whole crop of bad habits, none the less dangerous because they had been carefully pruned to deceive. Quinton at once took a deep interest in Margaret. The pretty trim girl in her orderly kitchen was a much pleasanter picture to contemplate than the draggle-tailed sluts with whom he had often indulged in clandestine gossip and joke. The dinner was now more savoury, the table more tempting. But innocent of the world's evil as she certain was, the scrupulous delicacy of discretion which was joined with her innocence kept Margaret as safe as was Spencer's Una with her lion in the wilderness. Quinton had in the past gone to the cupboard and helped himself to some lumps of sugar; now he found the cupboard door firmly locked. Margaret was always civil and kind but would never chatter and flirt and Quinton was profoundly disgusted to find that his days of surreptitious giggle had come to an abrupt end. His appearance in the kitchen did not make a pause in Margaret's industry. His compliments were received with sincere silence and his dubious wit was decidedly snubbed. He resolved to ask Margaret to go for a walk with him but somehow the overture died on his lips.

'It's an awful swindle!' he grumbled. 'To think that the very girl with whom a fellow would like to have some amusement is so set against it! This Margaret Ede would be a perfect paragon if she was not quite so straight-laced!' Poor silly Quinton is not the first who has thought something might be improved by an addition that would destroy it altogether. Those who will paint their roses blue must soon find themselves with nothing but a few dead leaves. And there is nothing more pitiful than the sight of a man's lingering admiration for a woman of whom his own weakness has made himself unworthy. The thought of her and how utterly she was above and beyond him could make him desperately miserable amid the coarse merriment of the music hall, but it could not keep him from it. He would sit in the gaudy theatre, scarcely conscious of the inane jokes sounding in his ears, a pale tragic figure as disconsolate as a ghost in the halls of the Inferno. Quinton Rendall was sinking lower—sinking but the more surely that he gave no alarm to those who might have held out a warning hand.

Margaret alone had her fears but what could she do? There was no help to be had from Mrs Brunton; she was not the kind of woman who could have sat beside a murderer's wife during the hour of execution; she was made for the gentler duties of life. In God's world, God needs His daisies as well as His palms; so Margaret made up her mind that her present duty was to pray for him, to be always kind and cheerful and yet firm and alert when he was inclined to mope about.

One evening there was a violent ringing at the bell. Margaret flew to answer the summons. It was Quinton and he pushed wildly past Margaret in a desperate frenzy. When he reached his room Margaret heard him lock the door with unnecessary vehemence. Next morning Margaret found Quinton in her kitchen. He turned towards her a face which bore evidence of a sleepless night.

'I'm here to say goodbye for ever. I am going far away from here but I could not go off without a word to you.' Quinton in his wretchedness had learned that the angels move among us always but we do not see them till our eyes are opened.

'I only wish I'd seen more people like you a little earlier in my life,' said Quinton, his face drawn and haggard.

'O Sir!' said Margaret, 'Troubles come to be conquered, not to conquer us. Settle down to work and work harder than ever; that is God's way of pulling us through our troubles.'

Quinton's grating laugh jarred Margaret to the very soul. 'It's too late. I'll tell you about it. I've been gambling lately and last night I lost money I had taken from Mr Brunton's till.' Margaret gave a gasp of dismay. 'There you are!' he cried desperately. 'I told you so.' He started towards the door, but Margaret's hand detained him.

'No it would not be right of me to let you go thus, now I know you have sinned against your master. But I must also help you to set it right. That is what should come after sin, not despair. I've got nearly seven pounds lying upstairs. . . .'

'No!' cried Quinton sinking his head on his arms. 'I have not sunk to be such a blackguard as that. And besides that is not enough. I stole eleven pounds nine shillings.'

'I will find that sum,' promised Margaret. 'You will have to repay me gradually and when you have done so I think you'll like to tell Mr Brunton about it,'

Quinton's face brightened. 'Thats capital! I own I'd like to make a clean breast of it. How do you always manage to hit the nail so very straight Margaret?'

She went upstairs and returned in a few minutes with her seven sovereigns and another six she had set aside for her mother.

'Now you must tell me what I should do,' said Quinton as he took the money.

'You must forget your ways and give mine a fair trial,' said Margaret firmly. 'You are not to go to any music hall or theatre; and keep apart from your old acquaintances. You must go to Church regularly and read a chapter of the New Testament every night before going to bed. I think also you should join some classes at the Institution; but don't do that only to please me.'

'What will please you will be sure to be good for me,' said poor Quinton. 'I solemly promise to do all these things.'

Quinton Rendall kept faith with Margaret and with himself. As soon as he had repaid the money he confessed his fault to Mr Brunton and emigrated to Tasmania. And so Quinton went out into the world an honest man. He will never be a saintly type of character, but henceforth he will be on the right side in life's battle between good and evil. He will be the ready helper of every sick man or weary woman or weeping child. He will do what he can for them until better help comes along. Thanks to Margaret, Quinton had found out the difference between downward and upward.

CHAPTER VI: A LIFE OF SELF RENOUNCING LOVE

 ne evening when Margaret came to ask permission to go out to visit Miss Newton she was surprised by Mrs Brunton's strange manner.

'Well Margaret,' said her mistress, 'no doubt Miss Newton has always been very good to you, but really—do you know whether she has anybody staying with her?'

'A strange woman opened the door to me the last time I called,' replied Margaret.

'Ah,' exclaimed Mrs Brunton. 'It may be that you were mistaken. It seems that a man is there. He was seen at one of the windows.'

'At any rate,' added Mr Brunton looking up from his newspaper, 'it is wisest for Margaret not to be so friendly with Miss Newton till we see how things go.'

Margaret turned pale. 'I know you mean kindly Sir, but if she's in trouble now it's not my time to fail her. I asked your leave to go to her, but now I must go whatever you say.'

'And I'll come with you, cried Emily, throwing down the latest novel she had been perusing. 'What is the use of reading about tragedies if we are to turn away our heads when there is the chance of seeing one in real life?'

'Dear dear!' sighed Mrs Brunton as the girls went out. 'That's the worst of good servants—they do push themselves forward and take airs.'

The two girls sped on through the streets and down the narrow passage to Miss Newton's house. As they made to enter the hall, somebody rushed past them in the darkness. They ascended the stairs silently and knocked—once—twice—thrice. The two girls looked at each other in the pale lamplight.

'Hark! was that not a sound from within?' whispered Margaret.

'I thought it was only the wind,' said Emily. 'But oh Margaret!—what is that streaming under the door?'

Margaret was never able to give a clear account of what followed the awful discovery. There was a nightmare of strange faces. The crash of a fallen door, and the vision of Miss Newton stretched on the floor with a bright stream of blood oozing from her death-white brow. There was a kindly doctor and many policemen, asking questions. A knock on the door and in came a woman whom Margaret recognised as the one who had admitted her the previous day.

'I left Miss Newton and the gentleman quite safe about an hour ago,' said the woman. 'I thought it safe to do so since he had been as mild as milk for several days.' She told the inspector that she was a nurse trained to manage dipsomaniacs and delirium tremens, and that she had been hired by Miss Newton to look after the gentleman, whom Miss Newton simply called Edgar.

Then Mr Bayes, Miss Newton's lawyer came in great haste, evidently deeply stirred. Two of the best nurses from the neighbouring hospital were hired and Margaret was to help them tend the injured lady. Mr Bayes informed the policeman that Miss Newton had long taken a deep interest in a miserable soul called Edgar Lane, an old family friend. After a wild and destructive youth, Lane had steadied up for years but lately he had 'broken out' again and Miss Newton had tried one plan after another to rescue the unhappy man from the vice that held dominion over him.

'Poor Lane,' said the police sergeant. 'So today he must have lost control and viciously turned on her. These are the puzzling kind o' folk, the drunkards. Why I've known a man go home drunk and batter his little girl to death with the bag of toys he had bought her earlier in the day when he was sober.'

When the policeman had gone Mr Bayes took the girls aside and told them Miss Newton's secret. 'She was a good daughter in her father's widowed house. And there was a young man who came a great deal about the house—one of two brothers. And this man, Edwin Lane—'

'What, *Edgar* Lane?' corrected Emily.

'No no. I'm making no mistake—Edgar was his brother. And Edwin Lane and Miss Newton loved each other. Some young people are romantic in silence, and Edwin waited until his circumstances might make him worthy of the father's approbation. Then suddenly his visits ceased and the place that had known him knew him no more. Miss Newton's father made no sign of noticing young Lane's absence, and as he did not appear to heed one or two remarks she made, she had nothing to do but endure in silence. She said that she would learn the reason some day and was sure that Edwin would need no forgiveness. For seven years father and daughter lived quietly together and then the father died. Amongst his papers was found an envelope addressed to his daughter, containing two letters. The first was from her father. It told how years ago a neighbour told him that the young man who was his daughter's suitor was a secret drunkard of the very worst type. Old Mr Newton had been terribly staggered by this and on finding that the boy's father had himself been a reformed drunkard, he wrote to Edwin peremptorily forbidding him the house, adding that the boy must be well aware of his reasons for doing so. In a postscript to the letter, written in an agitated hand, the old man asked his daughter how he could have known his neighbour had made a mistake between the two brothers? The other letter was to the father from poor Edwin as he lay dying in a lonely lodging. There was no reproach in it. He said he could not blame Mr Newton for banishing one who was drunkard's son and whose only brother Edgar had already fallen prey to the same vice. But now he sent his dying love to Miss Newton, saying that he should soon be safe, where no disgrace could overtake him.'

'Oh, poor Miss Newton,' wailed Emily. 'Oh, how did she bear it?'

'She said she thought she would become mad,' continued the lawyer. 'She was sure that what saved her was the dismissal of all her servants and her staying alone in the house, doing all the housework herself. She sought out the drunkard Edgar Lane and told him the whole story, which so impressed him that he imposed on himself a strict abstinence from which he only broke loose a few months ago. Miss Newton did all she could to help him and give him shelter when he was in need. All her money has gone on good works. She has worked for her own bread, and has persistently done her own house-work. *My house-work was my friend in my time of need,* she told me, *and I will not abandon it now*. But it looks now, Margaret,' continued the lawyer, 'that from now on she will need by her side such a good and faithful servant as you have proved yourself to be.'

CHAPTER VII: THE END—HER OWN GATES

 wo years had passed. Miss Newton had recovered but would always remain a frail invalid, often unable to leave her couch. She and Margaret had procured a pretty house in the country, Miss Newton occupying the second floor, while Margaret's savings in service, laid out with her good sense, furnished very prettily the first floor, which they found no difficulty in letting off profitably.

One day a stranger knocked at the door and said he wished to look at the apartments. He was a tall, fine looking man with the free air of a genial nature accustomed to command. He gave his name as Mr Kenneth Fraser from Tasmania and expressed himself as more than satisfied with the rooms.

'The strange thing about him is,' said Margaret, 'that I feel as if I have seen him before.'

" He wanted to tell her a story."

Mr Fraser spent many happy weeks there in a quiet atmosphere of unmercenary service and kindliness. As for Margaret, she strove for a long while to think that a peculiar attraction which the stranger had for her was simply due to the haunting sense of having seen him before. Such women as Margaret do not easily surrender their freedom of fancy and heart. But she had to yield at last.

There came an evening when he followed Margaret into the garden where she had chosen to sit at work. Mr Fraser stood beside her and his head was high among the blossomy branches of the little tree, so that his slightest motion sent the petals flying down over Margaret's dark grey dress. He told her of a young lad who had to leave his home. He told her of his dreary journey, and how he had for a travelling companion a young girl whose sweet face attracted him and whose gentle self-control and helpful ways seemed to him the fulfillment of his ideal, and just as they parted he had learned that her name was—Margaret Ede.

'So that was you,' she cried dropping her work upon her knee. 'I wonder I did not recognise you! I always remembered you.'

'Listen,' said he, 'I have not finished yet. I went away to the far land and worked hard and so prospered. But I was still alone. Whenever I thought of making a home for myself a vision of your face would rise before me and I knew that if I took another woman as my wife I should have to tell her that there was someone in the world whom I should have preferred before her, only that she was swallowed up and lost to knowledge amongst the millions of a far-off city. And a voice sometimes whispered in my ear, "Wait." And then, Margaret, through a chance meeting with a young emigrant called Quinton Rendall I learned where to find you; and I made up my mind to come home. I have come to fetch you. Will you come?'

And Margaret is now herself the mistress of a great colonial homestead where her faculty for 'getting things out of oneself' has abundant scope. There are children in the house now, and many servants who seldom leave without bearing with them some touch of the dutiful influence which pervades The Great Farm. There are visitors too—travellers searching for health, young colonists coming to seek a bright future, and sometimes to forget a past. And all remember their stay under the Frasers' roof as a bright spot in life. And surely if one had a world full of people like those one finds there, the Kingdom of God for which we pray would be set up at once, and all the world would be one great home, so that there would be no more 'strangers within the gates'.

 THE END

FROM GOLDEN WEDDING LETTERS TO 'WE TWA', NOVEMBER 1927

... housemaid at Haddo. I always remember how extremely kind you were. I have thought of you many times during the years. We were all so happy together with you ...

... Many girls who are naughty and mischievous directly an ordinary good lady speaks to them have a very soft spot in their hearts for you, for you know how we feel and think ...

... that I belonged to the Onward and Upward Association and it brought back memories of very pleasant evenings spent studying those sets of questions. I was in service in Glasgow and had one evening out in the fortnight and I just enjoyed finding the answers and I was successful too. I have several treasured books (*Ben Hur* etc.) given as prizes ...

... a number of years since I left your service but I often think of the happy days I spent at Haddo. I have pleasant recollections of all the kindness received from you, Lady Aberdeen, and your family. At Christmas time especially everybody was remembered with some suitable gift. I still have a fishing book which I got in 1902 ...

... when I look at your picture I see again your sweet face as on that first night we met. How lovely you were to me then—when few can understand the torture of the struggle that has to be borne—and have been ever since ... (See page 3)

... To congratulate you upon your Golden Wedding. From one of the girls who joined your Onward and Upward Movement in Cromar district in the early eighties. How much I was benefited by the subjects and gained a good few prizes ...

... I suppose the Onward and Upward Association is stopt now. I just did the Bible questions last year and sent them in but perhaps the competitions have stopt now there are so many other things to do and everything different. I have very happy memories of the old days ...

BIBLIOGRAPHY

ABOUT LADY ABERDEEN AND HADDO HOUSE

We Twa (autobiography) Lord and Lady Aberdeen 1923
More Cracks wi' We Twa Lord and Lady Aberdeen 1925
A Guide to Haddo House Archie Gordon, 5th Marquess of Aberdeen.
  National Trust for Scotland, 1981
A Bonny Fechter (biography of Lady Aberdeen) Marjorie Pentland 1952
The Canadian Journal of Lady Aberdeen 1893–1898 Editor John T
  Saywell 1960 (Champlain Society, Toronto)
The Music of the North (Haddo House Choral Society) Eric Linklater
  1970

GENERAL

A Woman's Place Ruth Adam 1975
Ordinary Lives 100 Years Ago C Adams 1982
Victorian Culture and Society Eugene Black 1973
Trade Unionism in Aberdeen 1878 to 1900 Kenneth D Buckley 1955
Useful Toil J Burnett 1975
A Woman's Work is Never Done C Davidson 1982
Girls Growing Up in Late Victorian and Edwardian England
  C Dayhouse 1981
The Victorian Woman D Crow 1971
Not in front of the Servants F Dawes 1974
The Victorian Country House M Girouard 1971
Life in the English Country House M Girouard 1978
Below Stairs in the Great Country Houses A Hartcup 1980
Life below Stairs F E Huggett 1977
The Victorian Household M Lochhead 1964
The Domestic Revolution T McBride 1976
Social Class in Scotland: Past and Present A Allan MacLaren (editor)
  1976
The Other Victorians S Marcus 1964
Victorian Patchwork C Pearl 1972
Human Documents of the Age of the Forsytes E Royston Pike 1969
History of the Girls' Friendly Society M N Stubbs 1926
Women's Magazines 1693–1968 Cynthia L White 1970

FICTION

Ellice Hopkins R M Barrett 1907
Esther Waters George Moore 1894
Below Stairs, Servants' Hall, etc. Margaret Powell
Lark Rise Flora Thomson 1939
Robert Elsmere Mrs Humphrey Ward 1888
Heir of Redcliffe etc. Charlotte Yonge 1853 ff.